Hate Is The Sin
*Putting Faces on the Debate
over Human Sexuality*

Hate Is The Sin
Putting Faces on the Debate over Human Sexuality

John S. Munday

Routledge
Taylor & Francis Group

NEW YORK AND LONDON

First published 2008
by Routledge
270 Madison Ave, New York, NY 10016

Simultaneously published in the UK
by Routledge
2 Park Square, Milton Park, Abingdon, Oxon OX14 4RN

Routledge is an imprint of the Taylor & Francis Group, an informa business

© 2008 Taylor & Francis
Printed and bound in the United States of America on acid-free paper by
Sheridan Books, Inc.

All Scripture verses are from *The Holy Bible, New Revised Standard
Version,* © 1989 by the National Council of the Churches of Christ in the
United States of America.

Cover Design by Marylouise E. Doyle

Library of Congress Cataloging in Publication Data
    Munday, John S.
    Hate is the sin : putting faces on the debate over human sexuality / John
S. Munday.
       p. cm.
    Includes index.
    ISBN: 978-0-7890-3638-4 (hard : alk. paper)
    ISBN: 978-0-7890-3639-1 (soft : alk. paper)
    1. Homosexuality—Religious aspects—Lutheran Church. I. Title.
    BX8074.H65M86 2008
    241'.66—dc22

                                                            2007046135

ISBN 10: 0-7890-3638-X (hbk)
ISBN 10: 0-7890-3639-8 (pbk)
ISBN 10: 0-2038-8935-5 (ebk)

ISBN 13: 978-0-7890-3638-4 (hbk)
ISBN 13: 978-0-7890-3639-1 (pbk)
ISBN 13: 978-0-2038-8935-0 (ebk)

For those whose faith compels them
to seek justice in the world.

ABOUT THE AUTHOR

John S. Munday has a Master of Theology degree from Princeton Theological Seminary (1988). He is also a lawyer, having a Juris Doctor of Law degree from DePaul University (1967). He has written *Justice For Marlys: A Family's Twenty-Year Search for a Killer,* published by the University of Minnesota Press (2004, paper 2006) about an equally compelling subject—the murder of his stepdaughter Marlys by a serial killer. Westminster/John Knox Press published his first book, *Surviving The Death of a Child,* in 1995 and his last book, *Overcoming Grief: Joining and Participating in Bereavement Support Groups* was published in June 2005, by ACTA Publishing Co. of Chicago.

CONTENTS

Vantage Point

by
Jack Munday

The walkway through the garden
is hosting a debate.
Colors from both sides of the path say,
"I'm so pretty, look at me."

On one side, the white peonies
and peach iris are separated
from the clematis vine's white stars
by giant horseradish leaves.
"We are the flowers
of your childhood,"
they shout.

The loyal opposition proposes pink
peonies bowing to pure purple Dutch iris
and taller flowering bronze iris
tipped with ruby.
"You planted us too,
because we're special,"
they cry.

If the gardener would speak, praise
like rain would fall on each flower.
From the patio, from her chair of rest,
she sees symmetry that blends, does not divide.

Prologue

A First Encounter with Hate

"I'm finished with sex. Now it's time for murder," I announced to several members of the Long Lake Lutheran Church in rural Isanti County, Minnesota.

It was early February 2005, and we had just completed a meeting with twenty parishioners discussing the concerns some had about our denomination's consideration of blessing same-gender unions and allowing those in such unions to serve as pastors of churches in the Evangelical Lutheran Church in America (ELCA).

I explained to a confused-looking parishioner that this meeting's focus on human sexuality was over, and now my wife and I would be going to the confirmation class. We had been asked to talk to the confirmands about the fifth commandment, "Thou shalt not kill," as part of a discussion on the Ten Commandments.

We knew about murder. In 1979, my wife, Fran, came home to find that her daughter Marlys had been violently attacked. It took us almost twenty years to find justice for Marlys, and we learned a lot about homicide in that time. We continue to speak and write on bereavement issues, helping others survive the death of a loved one. We say it is our ministry.

The meeting on human sexuality at Long Lake Lutheran had been called by a woman who had been active in the congregation for many years. She was worried that the denomination had not condemned homosexuality strongly enough. The group met in the fellowship hall, sitting at tables that had been pulled together into a large, oval shape.

I attended because Colleen Johnson, a friend whose son is gay and in a long-term relationship, had invited me. I was supposed to be Colleen's support. I felt pain for Colleen when one woman said, "It's our

Hate Is The Sin

children. It's our children. I'm not going to let my children learn that it is okay to be gay."

"Some people are gay from birth," Colleen replied. "We're supposed to welcome them into the church. Our mission statement says we are a welcoming church."

Another woman said, "Don't you want the church to represent what the Bible says?" She put her hand on her Bible in front of her. She and Colleen made eye contact; Colleen looked away.

During the meeting the idea of forming a task force to look for alternative affiliations other than the ELCA was discussed. The meeting ended when the whole group, except for Colleen and me, voted to take the idea of a task force to the congregation's annual meeting.

LET'S NOT ADJOURN UNTIL AFTER AUGUST

When I left the sexuality meeting, I took two versions of a resolution the participants intended to take to the Long Lake Lutheran Church annual meeting later that week. I knew the resolutions would disrupt the congregation. A man on the congregation's council had drafted one version and a third-generation member had drafted another. Both versions resolved that a task force be formed of seven "active and concerned" members to look into alternative Lutheran affiliations, such as Lutheran Congregations for Mission in Christ, and various other Lutheran church bodies. Word Alone, a movement within the ELCA, was also considered. All of these options are much more conservative than the ELCA regarding same-gender relationships.

What concerned me most were some of the "whereas" clauses. One set focused on the ELCA's previous vote regarding its relationship with the Episcopal Church. It was still a sore point with some ELCA members, who felt this gave more authority to bishops and Churchwide Assemblies. More troubling were the statements that the ELCA Sexuality Task Force "advocates 'going along' with compromise to Biblical truth for the sake of 'getting along,'" and "not enforcing direct and flagrant violations of the current 'Visions and Expectations' with meaningful discipline." The latter document spells out conditions that a candidate must agree to in order to be ordained and called to ministry.

To his credit, an active member of our church council insisted that the pastors be informed before anything like this be made public. "Surprising the pastors," he said, "is a slap in the face." The point was clearly a good suggestion, and before going to talk with the confirmation group, I made copies of each resolution and placed them under Senior Pastor Howard Skulstad's office door

After the confirmation class, I went home. I found out later that some of the group asked to speak with both pastors. There was a lot of tension, and at one point Pastor Skulstad asked if they wanted him to resign. They didn't and were very clear about that. A few days later, Pastor Skulstad and I had breakfast and he expressed relief that the controversy was not about him. Just about sex.

The following Sunday, February 6, 2005, Pastor Skulstad was ready for the debate. He had the congregation's mission statement prominently displayed, and he loudly emphasized "We welcome ALL people." During his sermon, he asked if our mission had changed. He said, "We need to see it every Sunday. Do we want to change it to say, 'we welcome ALL people who think like us?' I've heard it said I should preach the Bible. Well, here it is."

He told a personal story of feeling rejected in college when he wasn't selected to a fraternity. "We as a church can't reject people," he said. "It might have been Jesus." He referred to Matthew 25: "When you did it to the least of these, you did it to me."

Later that afternoon, Pastor Skulstad opened the Long Lake Lutheran annual meeting with prayer. The organist led us in the hymn *Bind Us Together, Lord.* The Council President led us through the order of business for the day, and things seemed calm as people conducted the business of the church. Then, near the end of the meeting, the husband of one of the resolution drafters asked to be heard. Rather than form the committee, however, he made a motion that the annual meeting not adjourn but agree to reconvene on Sunday, September 25, 2005, after the ELCA Churchwide Assembly in Orlando.

During the resulting debate, angry words were spoken, as some people quoted Bible verses and others replied, "cafeteria Christians can't pick which sin they hate." After an hour of what had turned into a painful back-and-forth disagreement, the motion to continue the meeting in September was defeated 94 to 35. Cooler voices had prevailed, and the vote seemed to indicate that those concerned about the ELCA sexuality policies were in the minority.

The response by that minority was to leave the church, taking their money and their anger elsewhere. Both resolution sponsors were among the first to leave Long Lake Lutheran Church.

WHY I WRITE ABOUT THE HUMAN SEXUALITY DEBATE

Human sexuality was never one of my issues. No one in my immediate family is gay, or if they are, they have not come out. But I have spent over twenty-five years working with the bereaved and learning to deal with my own bereavement over the murder of my step-daughter, Marlys Ann Wohlenhaus, in 1979, by a serial killer.

I have written on grief and crime issues, and have worked with mourners. So it is a legitimate question to ask, "Why would a man who spent decades working with grieving people, who is bereaved himself, be concerned with human sexuality and particularly the sexuality issues of gays and lesbians?"

My initial motivation was born after hearing people in my home church condemn homosexuality: "It's a choice and they just like it so much they won't change," or "The church has always condemned those people." I do not believe a congregation can be healthy if a significant number of the members put down and reject a group or class of people.

I've seen mourners destroy their lives with hate; I've attended bereavement support groups where many of the mourners refused to give up their tightly held anger and hate. Congregations and individual church members can just as quickly become victims of their own hate. I wanted to know why some of the people I worshiped with regularly acted so harshly. I didn't know if there were gays and lesbians in our congregation, but I did know that hate would poison the haters and do more harm to them than any gay or lesbian who happened to come their way. I don't want to worship where hate was so strongly against any one group.

I was further spurred on when I met Colleen Johnson and the "boys," as she calls her son and his partner; when I attended worship led by ELCA Pastor Mary Albing; and when I had conversations with many others whose sexuality is the object of hate. A funeral counselor in California who has been in a monogamous relationship for twenty-six years with his partner, told me that he was beaten twice by other youths when he was young. "They didn't know I was gay. I wasn't out. But they beat me, called me a faggot. They used their hate as a way to justify beating up a stranger," he said.

Because I have met people who have been hurt badly, in some ways as badly as the bereaved I have worked with, I found myself needing to understand the hate. I have seen a mother of a murder victim talk endlessly about the killer, not ever mentioning her child. I have seen how destructive hate can be, both for the victim but also for the one who hates others. Hate of homosexuals can also destroy lives.

I have another reason for writing this book. I studied theology at two seminaries as I struggled with questions about why young people die, whether from cancer, auto accidents, murder, or suicide. Why does one become a serial killer? Why do so many young people commit suicide? Why does one passenger in a car die when it slides off the road and another person in the car walk away? I asked, "Why, God?" I wanted to know why people hated others whose sexual orientation was different from their own. Was the sinner, or even just the sin, so bad? "Why God, is there hate?"

Judging from the widespread debate both inside and outside the church, I would like to know why some same-gender couples want the church to bless their relationship, and why other people in the same church want to keep them out of the pulpit. Are we reading the same Bible?

THE MAN IN THE MIDDLE

Pastor Mary Albing is on the ELCA Minneapolis Area Synod roster of ordained ministers. She is currently listed as on leave from call. She was called to serve as pastor at Church of Christ the Redeemer, Minneapolis, in 2003, but that call is not recognized by her bishop or the ELCA. Pastor Mary Albing is a lesbian in a committed relationship.

Under ELCA rules, a pastor on leave from call has three years to find a new position, either as a pastor, a chaplain, a counselor, a staff member serving a bishop, or a professor at a seminary. When Mary moved from her work as chaplain to take a call at Lutheran Church of Christ the Redeemer, Bishop Craig Johnson and the Minneapolis Area Synod Council put Mary on leave from call. Mary's three-year leave ended in May 2006. Bishop Johnson is seeking an exception to the rule and desires an extension of Pastor Albing's on-leave status from the ELCA Conference of Bishops. They have tabled the matter three times.

During the Minneapolis Area Synod Assembly in April 2005, various resolutions were presented for vote on the human sexuality issues before the ELCA. One, Resolution RC 2005-6, sought to reaffirm the current policies of the ELCA with respect to same-sex unions and ordaining persons in such relationships. The resolution's contact person and first speaker, Pastor David Glesne, described the resolution as seeking to maintain the status quo until "a reasoned biblical and theological basis for change" could be provided. "None," he added, "has yet been given." I appreciated his gentle manner and the lack of strident language that others, on both sides, used to drive home conclusions that gave little or no room for debate.

This book asks the questions: How do these debates affect the people in the pew or those who would be in the pulpit? How will the decisions change their lives? Will the Church divide over the debate? How is this debate similar to those in other denominations?

Answers to these questions are found in the stories of people whose livelihoods and lives are challenged by the Church and its followers. Stories such as Mary Albing who seeks to be a pastor while in a lesbian relationship; Jay Wiesner, a gay man whose congregation defied the ELCA by ordaining and installing him in an Extraordinary Candidacy Project ceremony; David Glesne who attempts to heal relationships with gays and lesbians and yet denies them ordination and a blessing of their cohabitation; and the struggle Bishop Craig Johnson faces leading the ELCA synod in which Mary, Jay, and David each serve a congregation. It is my hope that these stories, along with stories of others on both sides of the debate, will motivate readers to search for their own answers to these important questions.

Chapter 1

Where Does the Hate
Come From?

Colleen Johnson parked her red, four-door, Dodge Dakota pickup as close as she could to the door of Long Lake Lutheran Church in rural Isanti County, Minnesota. She slid off the bench seat, slammed the door shut, and marched to the house of worship. Shivering in the late winter wind, Colleen braced herself against the storm she would face inside.

In the sanctuary, other congregants were gathering to discuss human sexuality under the leadership of Associate Pastor Andrew Prin. The discussion followed the study published by the Evangelical Lutheran Church in America that deals with sexuality—in particular homosexuality in ordination and marriage. Under the present policy, celibate homosexuals may be ordained, but those in long-term relationships cannot be ordained or have the church bless their union. Colleen wanted to take part in the discussion because her son is in a fourteen-year relationship with his partner. A member of the church since 1977, she knew many in the congregation.

Colleen sat next to me in a pew and smiled at a woman she saw frequently at a weekly Bible study breakfast. Senior Pastor Howard Skulstad, balding and gray, and a man who radiates pastoral concern for his people, opened with a brief prayer, read Scripture, and led a recitation of the Apostles' Creed. The group of eighteen then walked from the sanctuary to the fellowship hall.

Pastor Prin, a large man admittedly overweight with an engaging smile, took his place at a podium to begin the evening's discussion. In this and the other sessions he led, Pastor Prin did a fine job of explaining the issues, using the ELCA supplied study guides. Pastor Prin explained the various translations of the word "abomination" as it had

Hate Is The Sin

been written in Greek and Hebrew. The group listened patiently to citations in the Old Testament book Leviticus. Pastor Prin read, "You shall not lie with a male as with a woman; it is an abomination" (Leviticus 18:22).

Colleen frowned when a woman she had known for years asked, "Well, if homosexuality is a sin, what is there to debate?"

A large, very overweight man said, "It's a sin, and those people love what they do. It's like me and food. I can't give it up."

Colleen noted the tone of those that spoke and would later tell me, "I find it hard to say you're a Christian if a person is so homophobic. I have a difficult time with those who are so sure they are right."

Pastor Prin asked the group to consider other things listed as an abomination, such as wearing clothes made from two different fibers or planting two different crops in one field. He remarked that if we used the Bible to accuse and discount one specific act, we should remember there are many other things also listed as abomination that our society embraced. He went to page six of the background essay to read more about the Leviticus texts. An argument has been made to ignore some of the texts on homosexual acts in present times because the texts focus on no longer practiced cultic prostitution. This argument met with great resistance from many in the group.

"Why would same-sex relations be the worship of fertility gods?"

"People choose to be gay."

During the discussion, Pastor Prin said he believed that there couldn't be "really meaningful dialogue" until the whole group agreed on whether homosexuality (or more precisely, a homosexual act) was a sin. Several people reaffirmed their belief that they can hate the sin and love the sinner. One long-time member of Long Lake Lutheran said, "Neutrality between good and evil is not possible."

Another woman, who has since left Long Lake Lutheran to join another church, spoke of hosting a niece and her lesbian partner for dinner. She said she loves her niece and had a wonderful time, but wanted to tell them they were living in sin. "The Bible says that is wrong, and if we stand by and let them do that, they'll go to hell," she said. Everyone who responded agreed with her, and even encouraged her to confront her niece.

Pastor Prin said, "If we have trouble within the family on this, how are we ever going to act with strangers?"

None of the voices speaking that night contained much love, and I wondered how Pastor Prin felt when he heard their anger. When Pastor Skulstad said, "My sin is food. I eat too much," a woman mocked him, shouting out, "Oh food, I love you so much!"

An older woman asked about tough love, especially on these issues. "The Bible says the homosexual lifestyle is wrong. It is a sin, and it says so plain and simple."

As if weary from the condemnation of homosexuality, Senior Pastor Skulstad asked, "How do we honor the body of Christ when we reject the honest opinions others have on this topic?"

Time after time people said, "But it's a sin," as though there is only one way to read the Scriptures. Someone asked if it is even possible for a gay person to find Christ. There seemed to be no room for anyone who had a different view, even when Pastor Skulstad said, "Lutherans see that the new law is 'to love God and love your neighbor as yourself.'" Like the incessant beat of a hammer hitting nails, people kept replying "But it's a sin."

As I sat there listening, I wondered if there was another way to find common ground between people with such polarized positions. As a person who has worked for more than twenty-five years with the bereaved, particularly with parents and siblings whose child or sibling has died an early death, I could not understand the hateful words of people who claimed to be Christian. I could feel the hate, but could not explain it. Could opposing groups talk to one another to understand their mutual humanity and to see the person instead of the sin or the homophobia? I wanted to find out. I needed to talk with people on both sides of the dialogue.

A number of people agree with Pastor Prin: we won't have peace in the church until those who are in favor of gay ordination and unions and those who are against them agree on whether or not homosexual acts are a sin.

At the time I disagreed. I thought peace would be achieved when people believed that others are entitled to valid theological and biblical interpretations different from their own, such as those who regard divorce as a sin and those who don't, or those who allow women to become ministers and those who don't. Later, when I came to understand this as a matter of justice and not biblical interpretation, I would see that the exclusion of women or divorcees or same-gender, faithful couples is simply not just.

The dialogue must continue. It is essential to know people as human beings–not as sinners to be judged and then dismissed.

IT'S ALL ABOUT SEX

I met with the Reverend Mary Albing, a pastor in the Minneapolis Area Synod of the ELCA who is listed on the roster of pastors as being on leave from call. She is also the pastor of Lutheran Church of Christ the Redeemer, in south-west Minneapolis, and lives in a long-term relationship with her female partner, Jane Lien. Mary was married for seventeen years and has a son and a daughter. She holds her ex-husband in high regard.

Pastor Albing met me in the entry hall of the church and welcomed me into her office with an impish twinkle in her eye. She closed the door, offered me a chair, and sat down.

"I'm glad to see you. How is Howie?" she asked, referring to mutual friend Pastor Howard Skulstad.

Her desk was cluttered as though she had been writing a sermon. We talked about the human sexuality issues facing the church.

"My congregation doesn't even think about me as a lesbian in the pulpit," she said. "Everyone in the pew has something she or he is struggling with, and suffering is our common ground in this church. Our similarity is suffering. One of the reasons I'm Lutheran is because this denomination is more attuned to suffering than most, and Lutherans take it seriously."

"How is your suffering redemptive?" I asked.

"I can't change my orientation," she said. "It is a given. I could choose to be celibate, and some ask me why I don't choose that option—if only to get a call. But there are other things you don't choose, such as your parents, how many siblings you have, being diagnosed with lung cancer when you didn't smoke—good and bad things. I want to help people find common ground. I'm convinced, when all is said and done, that our common ground is our suffering."

"So," I asked, "what about the Bible verses some people cite to condemn homosexuality? How do you deal with them? Or do you?"

Mary frowned. "On Biblical passages, it is hard, for example, to take a few verses from Leviticus seriously when we don't follow all the many, many other rules set out there. Context matters. Paul lived in a Roman and Greek culture where mentoring sometimes included pedophilic behavior, but didn't have anything to do with being gay. People at that time didn't think in the same categories we do. Paul looked at this behavior and saw the Greek and Roman culture doing things he thought were not natural. Sexuality, however, wasn't even a topic of study until after the 1940s. Now reputable sciences say that homosexuality is natural.

"But," she added, "for the sake of argument, what if we agreed that homosexuality is a sin? Romans says all sorts of things are sins, so why pick one? All have sinned. In Corinth, Paul wrote to a mixture of gentiles and Jews who were quarreling over one another's sins, arguing that we are all to be free in Christ to love our neighbor. When he wrote to Corinth, trying to help them be reconciled with one another, Paul challenged their judgments of one another and asked, 'What is beneficial for the congregation in Corinth?' As far as same-sex unions, blessings, and ordinations, we could ask what should take place now that would be most beneficial for the church or society? Paul talks about sin in order to help the people of Corinth get along, not to drive them apart. There are four hundred places in the Bible talking about love, and seven on gender."

"Then," I said, "we're not talking about one partner cutting the grass and another doing the dishes." Mary laughed when I said, "So it all boils down to the sex acts."

"That's about it," she replied. "In my congregation, which I admit is liberal, sexuality between committed partners is just not an issue. The point is their commitment. We look at God as so generous—what applies to the majority applies to all. Many people say that their minds were changed when they met gays and lesbians. You can't tell people it isn't a sin—they won't change their minds simply by you saying so—but give them a chance to know the humanity of others and they will change."

Mary has written a book titled *Called Into Ministry: To Be a Good and Faithful Pastor* (2005) that tells of her struggle to be such a pastor while acknowledging her relationship with her partner, Jane. Her book is her way of giving readers a chance to know her humanity.

I knew that both Mary and the Lutheran Church of Christ the Redeemer are at risk, depending on how the ELCA decisions are worded. A strict interpretation of the present rules could take away her status as a rostered pastor and could even lead to discipline against the congregation.

"Do you think acceptance will happen in time? For you, I mean. I understand you are in your third year on leave of call, and that at the end of the third year, the Bishop has to recognize your call or take you off the roster. What is going to happen to you, and to this congregation?" I asked.

"I wish I knew," she said. "Maybe we'll find out in Orlando at the 2005 Churchwide Assembly."

IT'S ALL ABOUT SIN

Pastor David Glesne is the senior pastor at Redeemer Lutheran Church in Fridley, Minnesota, just a block off East River Road that runs along the Mississippi River. Redeemer, founded in 1916, is a mature church whose congregation grew rapidly in the 1960s when the city of Fridley boomed. Redeemer has an average worship attendance of about 900 in the four Sunday services.

I met with David in his office in the newer part of the complex. He has served Redeemer for ten years and describes his ministry as the church being a huge ship anchored safely in a harbor. His role has been to head the ship out to sea, to rebuild the culture and environment, and once again follow the great commission. The church abounds in small groups, with almost 700 of the confirmed membership of over 1,300 meeting regularly in small groups.

"We also have a strong support of foreign missionaries at Redeemer," David said.

At a Minneapolis Area Synod Assembly earlier that year, David introduced a resolution calling for the church to keep its current standards for ordination and not make exceptions for persons in same-gender relationships. I told him that I was interested in his work to co-sponsor the resolution and asked if his church had used the sexuality study material.

"We had three sessions, with over one hundred in attendance each time. In the fall of 2002, I gave a series of twelve sermons on contemporary culture, such as sexuality, drugs, abortion, racism, and so on. Then we did the studies."

I told David about the hate I saw during those same studies at my church, and he said that his experience was different. "We have a very open discussion, and we are being faithful to Christ's call to offer hope to everyone. We are open and affirming, and this is who we have to be, need, and want to be. Just before you arrived," he added, smiling, "I met with a woman who says she is a lesbian. We meet once a month. We have good conversations."

"Yet you are not in favor of same-sex unions?"

"No," he replied, "but that's not the first issue. Everyone is a sinner, and the first thing we must do as Christians is to repent of our sins. Homosexuals have been rejected by large parts of society, and when they came to church, they felt rejection there. Now they've gone to other church organizations, outside the ELCA. We haven't been Christ to them."

"Where does the hate come from?" I asked.

David looked troubled and said he had done soul-searching on that topic. "When homosexuals come to the church, they find rejection and go somewhere else. That is wrong. The first step is for us Christians to repent our sins, for all the hatred. We have wronged gays and lesbians and haven't been Christ to them. The Bible isn't homophobic," he added, now smiling, "but speaks out against homosexual activities opposite of God's statutes."

David has also written a book, titled *Understanding Homosexuality: Perspectives for the Local Church* (2005). I bought a copy from him in anticipation of a continued dialogue.

IS IT OKAY TO BE DIFFERENT?

I assumed that it is more difficult to hate someone who attended worship with one's family than it is to hate a stranger. I contacted a woman who serves on my home church council and who is a very active member. I invited her and her daughter to talk with me.

"When I sat through Pastor Andrew's sessions," the mother said, "I felt the vicious attacks. Hateful people. I decided, 'I'm going to give homosexuality a face.' I wanted release of what is bottled up inside me. I am doing this to feel better. So I told them that my daughter is living with a woman in a partnered relationship. They are lesbians."

The daughter was confirmed at Faith Lutheran Church in the city of Isanti, but when her parents moved she joined Long Lake Lutheran Church and sees it as her home church. She is optimistic about being accepted and would not expect anything less.

She shared, "I would feel like I was lying if I wasn't honest. I want to get my life together and don't want to lie when I go through an adoption and I want children. It is not like I chose it or could be healed."

In 2003 at age twenty-nine, she came out after having made a commitment to her partner. She had been engaged twice before to men, but ran from both engagements.

"They were nice guys, but I didn't feel anything. I went to church quite a bit, but I began to wonder, 'Who do I make happy? Everyone else or me?' I have always known I am different, but I tried to fit in."

"Why are so many people filled with hate?" I asked her.

"They are afraid," she said, "like maybe accepting gays and lesbians might put the idea in their head that it is okay to be different."

"But," I said, "that presupposes a choice."

"It isn't." She shifted in her chair from one armrest to the other. "Homosexuality looks so much different on the other side. I've been over there, and I know what they see. I used to dream I was a boy because that was how I looked at girls. I would cry, 'Why God don't you make me a boy?' I had my first boyfriend at sixteen, and all I got out of it was to wear his class ring and say, 'Look at me.' I didn't realize it, but I looked at girls in movies and didn't know it was wrong. I saw where clothing was too tight or loose and had many major discussions with God. I'm different from what everyone is comfortable with."

Chapter 2

A Church Ahead of Its Time

The Lutheran Church of Christ the Redeemer is an ELCA congregation in South Minneapolis that has a reputation for being liberal
and ahead of its time. With a small congregation of about 200 baptized members, its average attendance on Sunday is about 100. LCCR
is the church where Pastor Mary Albing works and where the congregation anxiously watches the on-goings of the ELCA on matters such
as human sexuality. It is a congregation at risk.

LCCR began studying issues of human sexuality back in 1975 under then-pastor Rick Foss who was the first pastor of what was a two-
point Southwest Lutheran Parish where LCCR shared ministry with
nearby St. Andrew Lutheran Church. Pastor Foss served from 1971 to
1977, and left to work in Fargo, North Dakota, as an associate pastor.
He has since become Bishop in the Eastern North Dakota Synod of
the ELCA. His successor, Pastor Jarvis Streeter, stayed just fifteen
months and left when the LCCR congregation decided to leave the
two-point parish. Pastor Donald J. Luther, initially called to tend
the church in the face of expectations that it might not survive, led the
congregation for nearly twenty-two years.

In 1990, long before this congregation was ready to call a partnered lesbian as its pastor, the ELCA released a human sexuality
study. Pastor Don Luther led this small but vibrant congregation that
took an interest in many of the issues confronting the ELCA and
Christians everywhere. It is, for example, in a sister-parish relationship with Christmas Lutheran Church in Bethlehem, Palestine.

When I asked Pastor Don Luther about his views on homosexuality, he said, "I have an assumption that almost everyone on this issue
experiences change. The way one moves from not liking homosexuals (I won't say 'homophobic') to accepting them is when someone
important to them turns out to be homosexual."

Hate Is The Sin

Don told of a woman who attended Hamline University in St. Paul during the 1950s with his wife. This woman was disabled from polio, and over the years led the American Lutheran Church (before its merger into the ELCA) in disability gains. She made a major impact. Don also got to know her.

In Don's second year at LCCR, there was a program on human sexuality for the staff where his wife worked and the spouses went as well. The title was Sexual Attitudes Reexamined. On Thursday of the week-long event, those who wanted to went to dinner at the home of a homosexual couple. That next Saturday, Don and his wife were talking in the kitchen when their thirteen-year-old son came in and heard them say they enjoyed the evening with the gay couple. He asked if that was true.

"Yes," Don said.

"My friend's father is gay," his son commented.

"What do you think?"

"He's a nice man," the son said, and went back to what he had been doing. To Don this meant that his son had not been programmed to dislike gays. After the conference, the disabled friend came out to Don's wife, and later to Don. She and her partner had established a long-term relationship together.

Don admits he has not always been fair to gays and lesbians. In 1988, a woman parishioner came into the outer office. The door was open and Don was on the phone talking with another pastor and said that his sister couldn't believe how the lesbians were hitting on her. He admits he said some awful things in very bad humor. After the call, he stepped out to greet the woman who said, "I heard you. Do you remember that my daughter is lesbian?"

Don grimaced even after such a long time had passed. "I couldn't even say I was sorry. I just asked for forgiveness. We got along after that, and we worked well together on church things over the years."

"This is what you meant about experiencing change," I said. "Thank you for the personal and painful example."

In 1990, LCCR had a four-week series on human sexuality and Don decided to teach the fourth week, on the biblical teachings.

"The first week there were twenty-five, and by the end of the series fifty-five were in attendance, compared to eighty at Sunday worship back then. The tapes are still in the church library. When another ELCA Sexuality Study was published, it hit the church like a bomb."

Don had six two-hour sessions of fifteen to twenty people, and tried to display himself as being open. Then he was asked by his friend and her partner, "Would you do a same-sex union service?"

"I am very conservative about marriage, and require every couple to have some connection to the church," Don said. "At least one has to be a member. So I said I would perform a blessing if they were willing to go through the same procedure as straight couples. That included counseling.

"They left and I thought that was the end of it. Two weeks later they came back and said, 'We'll do whatever.' I gulped and said, 'Okay, but you can't call it a marriage.' I said a wedding is an exchange of promises, prayers, blessing, set in the context of the Eucharist, so this can be a service of thanksgiving. I met four times with the couple and covered the same stuff as always. It was my agenda that the vows had to be unconditional, and I got to edit them. I didn't want psychobabble. Then I went to the church council, who approved, reminding me that the two women were members after all." I saw that Don took pride in their reminder.

Don smiled at another memory. "Before the service, I went to the bishop of the Minneapolis Area Synod and met him in his office. We went to seminary together and I said I was telling him what I was doing, not asking for permission.

"He may have been provoked by my not coming sooner. Then he laughed, asked if there were banns published, which there were, and a center aisle procession, and vows, and so on. He said, 'If it walks like a duck, and quacks like a duck. . .' and we both laughed. Over one hundred came to the service, including twenty-five from our congregation."

There was a subsequent controversy, Don explained. "At the June Council meeting, we invited anyone who wished to do so to sit in. There were ten on the council and sixteen others came raising questions. There was one fundamentalist who bossed his wife and kids, and said, 'We're leaving this church and you're all going to hell.' One other family left."

AFTER DON, THEN WHO?

Don explained that the congregation of LCCR decided to become a Reconciling In Christ (RIC) church. A member of LCCR belonged to the group that advocates a welcoming and accepting attitude toward gay, lesbian, bisexual, and transgendered (GLBT) persons. She urged the congregation to accept the principles of RIC. After some discussion Don said LCCR would not join unless the name was changed from "Reconciled" to "Reconciling," because to claim being fully reconciled in Christ presumed too much. In 1995, the church council decided to have a congregation vote on RIC, but stipulated the need for at least 60 percent of the votes to pass. RIC was approved by an even larger margin than 60 percent.

"I planned to retire in September 2001. LCCR tends to have a significant number of strong-willed people and a disproportionate number of strong leaders. It is also a church in transition; it started as a largely neighborhood congregation in 1943 and it continues to become much more diverse. In 2002, only forty-five member households were in the three local zip codes surrounding the church, while fifty-seven households were located in metro-wide diversity and another thirteen outside the Minnesota metro area."

Don announced his forthcoming retirement in May of 2001, and held a forum. "I told them, 'This is what I want to do' and then explained what the call process would involve. Someone brought up the Extraordinary Candidacy Project and asked, 'Do you think we can explore that?' and I said yes."

Following Don Luther's departure, and still early in the service of an interim pastor, members began talking about the search for a new, permanent pastor. Some members asked how a Reconciling in Christ congregation, with a commitment to full participation in the life of the church for GLBT persons, could exclude from consideration for pastoral call those persons who cannot be on the ELCA clergy roster because of same-gender relationships, though they are otherwise qualified to serve in Lutheran pastorates.

The congregation council proposed discussion of a change in the LCCR constitution to allow consideration of persons on the Extraordinary Candidacy Project (ECP) list. These are persons who are fully qualified to serve as Lutheran pastors, except they are not in compliance with the "Visions and Expectations" requirement that they be either married (heterosexually) or celibate. The council arranged a special meeting with Minneapolis Area Synod Bishop Craig Johnson and one of his staff associates to discuss the implications of a constitution change. In that discussion, the bishop said he could not officially recognize a call from the ECP roster. He mentioned no disciplinary sanctions that might be taken against the congregation, essentially remaining non-committal on the question.

After the congregation voted to make the constitution change, a call committee was elected and started its work in September 2002. A number of candidates were proposed by the synod office, several more from the ECP roster applied, and there were also nominations by LCCR members directly.

Council President Ruth Ann Peterson remembers that there was a lot of discussion on the ECP issue—not about whether a change in LCCR's constitution was right or wrong–but what would happen and how might the church be jeopardized by the change. In theory, the church could be at risk of censure, sanctions, or even removal from the list of ELCA congregations if it went too far in skirting the call process as defined by the ELCA. Nevertheless, LCCR did change its constitution (by a vote of 64 to 9), allowing consideration and possible call of a pastor on the Extraordinary Candidacy Project list. As Ruth Ann recalls, "It wasn't that we had to have someone from that list. We just simply didn't want to exclude anyone. What else is the point to be Reconciling in Christ?"

WHAT TO DO WITH MARY?

The Congregation Mission Profile was prepared by the call committee and the council president. The Profile noted three developments that were important in the church's history. One stated that there had been a strong growth in "Centrality of Sacramental Life," which included every Sunday Eucharist and meaningful physical acts such as cross-signing and touching water of the baptismal font when entering church. Another development focused on a strong commitment to social justice and peace, highlighting what the committee felt was an evolution from a traditional Lutheran stance of individualism and quietism on political questions into a "forthright emphasis on linking faith and public life." Not surprisingly, these two developments framed the third development: a concern for the relationship between the church and homosexual persons. On this third development, the Mission Profile says:

Study and Actions on Human Sexuality. Starting with a 1975 weekend sexuality seminar, which Pr. Rick Foss later said was "the most remarkable thing that happened during my six years there." This agenda continued in the 1980s and '90s with major education attention to the church and homosexuality, involvement of numerous members in synodical work on gay-lesbian concerns, public worship blessing of a lesbian committed relationship, becoming a Reconciling in Christ congregation, and (in 2002) decision to amend constitution to permit consideration of Extraordinary Candidacy Project candidates.

The Mission Profile states that the only significant conflict in LCCR's past two decades has been the attention the church placed on relationships involving gay and lesbian persons. The profile conceded that several households left in 1993 because of the church's public blessing of a lesbian relationship, and suggested that others may have left due to discomfort with LCCR stances on sexuality and social concerns generally.

The profile stated that issues on which members disagree need not be avoided but should be dealt with openly, honestly, respectfully, and over an extended period of time. It seemed clear that those who stayed at LCCR knew how to get along even when they had different opinions on sensitive subjects. The eighteen-page document set the stage for the quest to find LCCR's new pastor. And they did.

In the 1990s, Pastor Mary Albing worked in a 3,000-member church in Grand Forks, North Dakota, on the staff with her husband, Pastor Bob Albing. Jane Lien was single, a friend of Bob and Mary, and of their children. Mary's work at the church was too stressful, and the family moved away, becoming co-pastors of a Lutheran church, St. Peder's, in south Minneapolis.

During these years Mary spent two years in counseling, then told Bob she was lesbian. They stayed together for three more years, struggling to make sense out of their relationship. During that time, Mary had questions about her integrity. She saw her marriage become a mockery of what she had thought marriage was supposed to be. Finally, the couple agreed to a divorce.

Many people asked, "How did you not know about your own sexuality?"

Mary felt that she couldn't tell her congregation. Maybe later, after she had left, they would learn of her reason for not staying at the church. That would be hard enough for some members. She left to be a chaplain at Abbott Northwestern Hospital in Minneapolis. When Mary went through her divorce, she went to Bishop David Olson. Bishop Olson was then Bishop of the Minneapolis Area Synod. She talked to her bishop and she remembers that he told her to, "Tell all. Divorce happens."

Then she told him why she and Bob were getting the divorce and he said, "Sometimes we have to keep things secret." Mary Albing remained on the ELCA roster of ordained pastors.

Mary missed parish life. She also affirmed her relationship with Jane Lien. Mary read a book by Wayne Muller, *How Then Shall We Live* (1996). One of the chapters encourages readers to pursue their vocations, asking them the question, What Do I Love? So inspired, Mary filled out mobility forms, which alert the bishop that a pastor is ready to take a different call. When Mary came to the question about whether or not she intended to remain celibate if unmarried (to a man), Mary wrote "no," explaining that she felt she kept the expectations as well as any other pastor, with very few exceptions, but believed that the intent is to keep gay people from serving the ELCA. Visions and Expectations states single and gay people must be celibate, but has a number of other parts, such as a promise to be a good steward and support the church. Her response led to a conversation with newly installed Bishop Craig Johnson.

The "Visions and Expectations" language of significance is, "Ordained ministers who are homosexual in their self-understanding are expected to abstain from homosexual sexual relationships." Sixteen words out of over 5,500. Bishop Johnson telephoned Mary, and at the end of the conversation said he believed she was a good pastor, but he would not sign her call papers if she received a call.

As it happened, the cantor at LCCR knew of Mary through contact with Jane Lien. He recommended her to LCCR's call committee, who subsequently asked her for her mobility papers.

The co-chair of the call committee took the papers, thinking it was probably too late to consider Mary. "But it wasn't," Ruth Ann has since said. "Mary was so at the top of our total list of candidates that the call committee recommended we call her." Members of the call committee concluded that Mary had the qualities they sought–almost a perfect match. The congregation voted to call Mary by a margin of 58 to 17. The Synod didn't approve the call but has since not taken any further action against LCCR, keeping Mary on the roster of pastors on leave from call.

On May 18, 2003, LCCR installed Pastor Mary Albing as its pastor. Taking part in the service were three retired bishops of the ELCA—Lowell Erdahl, David Brown, and Darold Beekmann. Each affirmed Pastor Mary. Former Bishop Darold Beekmann preached the sermon, and said, "To have the audacity to risk fully, to not be afraid what the consequences might be, but not be naïve about what those might be, is to live out the Gospel."

Council President Ruth Ann concluded the ceremony saying, "With great joy and gratitude, on behalf of the Lutheran Church of Christ the Redeemer, I welcome you as our pastor."

Others were not so welcoming. Several conservative organizations have been critical of LCCR's actions, citing Scripture and tradition as the basis for denying Mary the opportunity to serve as a pastor while in a relationship.

Although Bishop Craig Johnson did not sign the letter of call and has kept a copy in his files, he and the Minneapolis Area Synod Council have not taken any further actions against Mary or the congregation. Mary and Bishop Johnson have continued a dialogue since her installation in 2003. Bishop Johnson has kept Mary on the Minneapolis Area Synod Roster with "on leave of call" status. Under normal circumstances, Mary's on leave status should have expired in May 2006.

Chapter 3

In the Eyes of God and Our Friends

The man who preached at Mary Albing's installation at LCCR, Darold H. Beekmann, is a retired ELCA pastor and former bishop of the Southwest Minnesota Synod. It is a synod in a conservative rural area where tradition and family values are less likely to change than in the more progressive metropolitan regions of Minnesota. Darold also served as president at the Lutheran Seminary in Gettysburg, Pennsylvania.

I met Darold's son, Tim, on a Sunday afternoon in Minneapolis. Tim was giving a talk to a support group for families of gays and lesbians. We met in the lounge of the University Lutheran Church of Hope. A circle of comfortable chairs faced the fireplace and the speakers. A table had been set up for sign-in sheets and nametags. Other tables had refreshments and a lending library.

After the facilitator gave opening announcements and a prayer, Tim took his place in front of the group. Because I didn't know Tim, or his father and mother, I was briefly surprised to see that Tim looks African American. He is the Beekmann's adopted son.

Tim grew up in Willmar, Minnesota, and was one of two black people in town. His father was the pastor of a local Lutheran church, which gave him some support. Still, he struggled at dating time. Tim explained that college was a fresh start for him. At college he developed a relationship with a female classmate, and eventually they became engaged and began planning their wedding. Tim began asking himself, Who am I?

"I didn't want to be different again and face another round of discrimination, but I also wanted to be honest. I was tired of denying my sexuality. To be fair to my fiancée and myself, I decided not to go ahead with the marriage. Later I told my parents and they were very supportive."

Hate Is The Sin

"Several years later, mutual friends introduced Patrick and me. We were quickly attracted to each other, discovering that we have much in common. In time we had a commitment to each other. We wanted to be held to the same standard of commitment as those who are allowed to make that commitment in the church. We are not legally married, but we are in the eyes of God and our friends."

Tim's mom, Marlene Beekmann, stood next to her son. Throughout Tim's childhood, Marlene had witnessed the discrimination aimed at him because he was part black. She said that Tim didn't always want help. "Now," she says, "people asked me, 'Isn't it hard that he's gay?' and I said, 'No. He's my son and nothing could make me love him less. He's the same Tim I have always known.' Both Tim and Patrick grew up in the church and they wanted the people to witness their commitment. During the commitment service at Edina Community Lutheran in suburban Minneapolis, many in the congregation were crying or smiling out of joy. They didn't see two men, they saw two baptized children of God committing themselves to a life-long relationship."

I watched this loving mother speak of her son: adopted, biracial, gay. Life for everyone would be better if they had such loving and accepting parents.

She had more to say. "One time when Tim was about five, he was at church. A woman came up to him and said, 'Little boy, you should not be running in the church, you should run at home.' Tim thought for a moment, then looked up at her and said, 'But I am home.'

"I was worried," Marlene added, "that after we're gone Tim would be alone. I'm not worried now. Tim and Patrick have each other. We can die in peace."

Darold Beekmann spoke with pride about the commitments made by Tim and Patrick. "Planning the service," he said, "and reflecting on its meaning were very special. They said, 'I love you and I want to spend the rest of my life with you.' I quote Patrick when I ask, Can that ever be bad? When they lighted the unity candle, it also reminded us that something is at work here that is bigger than sexual orientation. There are so many stereotypes that are wrong. Theirs is like all good relationships, based on faith, commitment, and love. Tim and Patrick are blessed. I feel sorry for church people who can't accept this, and thereby deprive themselves of the gifts and commitments as well as the faith and insight of gay people."

"The commitment service also led me to reflect on the significance of Marlene and me commonly being known as 'Marlene and Darold.' After the service everyone knew who Tim and Patrick are. That doesn't have to be explained anymore, and for some who still don't accept them, that remains their problem. We won't let it be our problem."

Tim, who had remained in front of us as his parents spoke, added, "Patrick and I have lived in a bubble. For example, we didn't know how the neighborhood would react, but they have been supportive and affirming. I'm leaning more toward speaking out because we have to educate people. Can't you see that those gays who want a church ceremony are more likely to stay together than those (straight people) who don't bother with the church's blessing?"

Talking with Tim and Patrick and retired Bishop Beekmann gave me a very different perspective than the conventional view of gays having many partners. They also put a different view on reading the Bible. The starting point may be where the author's world view is taken into account. If, as many say, "The Scriptures are divinely inspired," I wonder if that means that the author of Leviticus knew, or did not know, that in the present time there could be men like Patrick and Tim? These two men have said, "We have a commitment and want to be held to the same standard of commitment as straight couples." As Darold Beekmann asks, "Can that be bad?"

GOD DIDN'T STRAIGHTEN OUT THAT WORLDVIEW

I later met Darold to talk about his views on human sexuality. I was curious because he is the father of a gay man whose union was blessed in a church, and also because Darold took part in the installation of Pastor Mary Albing. I also knew that he had dealt with these issues as a bishop.

We met at a coffee shop in south Minneapolis. Darold warmly greeted me, took my arm and steered me to a table. He had a briefcase full of books with him and seemed very open to talk.

"The Bible," he said. "So often people read into it and see what they want to see. Back when I was in seminary, human sexuality was not addressed as a major issue, and I simply understood that there was an order of creation established by God, and to violate it is out of order. I read Genesis, portraying the dynamics of two becoming one—personal as one—and the implications of that for our life.

"The bottom line is fidelity and commitment. The power of Genesis 2 is its emphasis on 'to cleave' and the capacity to be totally validated in this most intimate, life-long relationship. We need to wrestle seriously with the many implications of this text for our understanding of marriage, but we also need to acknowledge that this text was not written to address the issue of homosexuality."

"Some," I said, "read Genesis to say that this establishes God's will for humanity; that a male and a female should join together. What about that?"

"Essentially I agree with that understanding. But this text does not rule out other possibilities, for example, those who are single, those who are celibate, and I would include homosexuals. The Bible was written to reveal God's redeeming work in the world. It is not a history book or science book, and many things are not addressed there. That which is addressed is in the context of God's saving activity. God's focus is on revealing his will and purpose. Genesis describes creation as a dome over a flat earth. God didn't bother to straighten out that worldview, but we understand the world is a globe spinning in space, circling the sun." Darold laughed. "Even those who most adamantly insist on a literal interpretation are not literal in every instance."

I hadn't had an issue with a flat earth before. "By that do you mean that since the world is a sphere, we can't read that literally and shouldn't read any of Genesis as a literal statement of fact?" I asked. "We should read it like a theology book?"

"Almost. The Bible should be read as a theology book, but it uses a variety of literary forms. To take the Bible seriously we must also take seriously its intentional use of these various forms. It doesn't attempt to project a scientific worldview. It proclaims that the purpose of all is to praise the deity, God, as portrayed in the Judeo-Christian faith. In Genesis 1 and 2, God declares this creation to be good, and describes it in order to explain its purpose.

"Genesis 1 was written during the exile in Babylonia where there was widespread belief in a plurality of gods, and that creation occurred as the result of a good god defeating an evil god. Genesis 1 addresses this belief system, using the language and structure of worship to assert that the God of Israel created the world out of chaos and established a created order. With a touch of humor, the text asserts that God created the other gods too. If you use texts for other purposes, you lose the sense of what they say and what they were written to address."

Darold opened his briefcase and sorted through the books. "Genesis 2 was written earlier, when Israel had power and wealth and yet the people felt unfulfilled and dissatisfied," he said. "They were culturally and spiritually bankrupt. They needed to be reminded that they were created by God to live in a relationship of dependence on God and not on 'stuff.' This relationship of dependence is concretely illustrated. The description of the fall in Genesis 3 portrays sin as rebellion against that relationship with God. To apply these texts to homosexuality is not right. Homosexuality is not even remotely addressed in Genesis 2 and 3."

"Then why," I asked, "do people read Genesis to condemn homosexuality, and particularly when it is a committed relationship and not a wild, adulterous lifestyle?" I was taking notes as fast as I could.

As I paused, the former bishop smiled. "I think, they are," he held up one finger, "one, often irrational, a gut reaction against something they have become ingrained to believe is wrong. Two," another finger, "some find it hard to believe in what they cannot prove, sometimes confusing faith and reason. The Bible is understood as the word of God, and not taking it literally is threatening to their faith. Faith is a leap—a belief in what we can't prove. Some need black and white answers rather than taking that leap."

Three fingers. "Fear is so often based on what is irrational. Four, faith shapes our personal identity, which makes changing views associated with faith so threatening. It is so much less threatening to read literally those texts that support our views. Our western minds tend to think abstractly. The Hebrew mind tends to think concretely. If the father ate garlic and the mother ate onions, you couldn't expect the son to smell of sweet perfume. That saying conveys a very concrete, profound truth which loses its meaning if interpreted literally.

"Five," he said, holding up his hand, "people are not comfortable with sexuality as a topic in general. Six, gays have been so heavily exploited for political purposes that it has almost made people hysterical. Political positions also shape personal identities, and when a particular position is challenged, it feels like the personal identity has been challenged."

He shrugged and looked directly at me. "That's a lot of reasons, but I have been dealing with this for a while now, and I'm not happy that there is so much irrational talk about sexuality." Darold looked sad now, and perhaps tired.

I thought of those who say we should love the sinner and hate the sin. "Some say there needs to be a new way to read the Bible that is biblically and theologically sound."

"Much of that work has already been done," he said. "But there is more. For example, the Book of Acts and some of Paul's letters offer rich insights into how the early church dealt with emotionally charged issues such as the requirement of circumcision and purification and the prohibition against unclean food. These things were deeply embedded in the faith and identity of Jewish Christians. Both sides of the current debate have missed the insights of these texts.

"Notice that Peter and Paul and others, including the councils in Jerusalem, didn't force the use of isolated Scripture texts out of context to avoid wrestling with the challenge and complexity of what these old practices meant for their new life in Christ. These New Testament texts don't offer quick and easy answers, but they do provide a helpful model for how the church can be open and faithful to the spirit's leading as it encounters new issues and circumstances in its life of Christ. There is so much to be learned from how the early church dealt with its issues. I had hoped the ELCA Task Force on Sexuality would incorporate some of these insights, but the Task Force missed it.

"As Lutherans we always say that for Luther, 'Scripture is its own interpreter.' No one text is understood apart from the whole, and one can't isolate one text. Scripture is the cradle of Christ. Scripture won't save you, but it is what brings you to Christ who does save you. Christ came to fulfill the law and prophets and take it to another level."

I felt that I was sitting with a wise, kind man who carried the weight of the ELCA's struggle with human sexuality. Still, I thought, a bishop at heart. "Well then are you satisfied that under some circumstances, being in a same-gender relationship is within the teachings of the Bible? I mean, you preached at Mary Albing's installation at LCCR, and your son Tim had his covenant relationship with his partner Patrick blessed in your church."

Now he smiled and relaxed. "The service was beautiful. Tim and Patrick had the structure, substance, prayers, hymns, and context of a marriage."

I THINK I KNOW THIS MAN

When I started to look for more opportunities to talk with people about human sexuality and the hate that I had seen and heard, I saw a notice of a Pride Interfaith Celebration at First Universalist Church, on Dupont Avenue in south Minneapolis. The meditation would be given by Jay Wiesner, pastoral minister of outreach at Bethany Lutheran Church in Minneapolis.

His name seemed familiar. Then I remembered that I knew Jay because we both served on the ELCA's Minneapolis Area Synod Council as lay people. I had no reason to know that he was gay, as that never came up in the conversations we had or in the remarks he made in the Council meetings.

I found the church, parked, and began to walk to the front door. Others nodded to me, smiled, welcomed me. I felt strange, not afraid but clearly different. Would someone think I'm gay? Would someone take a smile as interest? I know now that my nervousness was based on ignorance.

For whatever reason, I have never noticed people who, if someone points them out, appear to be homosexual. I didn't notice two males if they were holding hands or two females walking arm in arm, but just saw people. Here at First Universalist, I knew I would be seeing people whose sexual orientation was different from mine. Out of great ignorance, I didn't know how to react.

I saw Jay Wiesner putting on an alb and stole in preparation for the service. He seemed happy, smiling and nodding to people who walked past him.

I went into the sanctuary and sat in a pew. I looked around and saw people sitting together. Some couples were male, some female, some were a man and a woman. I turned my attention to the music being played. The sanctuary buzzed with energy. People continued to find their place in the pews.

The service opened with a praise band. The co-pastors of the church gave a greeting. A Jewish cantor sang the invocation, a Zen teacher in training read from writings by the Buddha, a Lutheran pas-

tor read from Genesis, and a choir from a Methodist Church sang. Jay
Wiesner began his sermon.

Jay opened by acknowledging that he hoped he wouldn't acciden-
tally step on the beliefs of others, noting that it was a very diverse
group, not just Christian. The biblical text he selected in Genesis,
Chapter 32, described how Jacob would not let go of the man he
wrestled with, God, Jay called him, until the man blessed Jacob. Jay
went on to say that people of faith, those in attendance, wrestle with
God, down and dirty, touching.

"As queers," he said, "the first person one wrestles with is one's
self, then with the family of origin. So many of us have heard, 'What
did I do to make you that way?' or 'No son of mine is going to dirty
our family name' and so on."

Jay pointed out how the gay community is so divided on opinions,
including same-sex marriage, that it really isn't the dreaded mono-
lithic gay agenda that others fear. "Queers wrestle with God, ponder
and struggle. We, too, won't let God go, and God won't let us go. The
radical hope is that there will be a different world, and that is what
they hope for."

Jay's face shone with excitement and a little sweat as he closed,
saying, "Who are you afraid to wrestle with? May God give you that
hope to go to the wrestling mat."

On the way home, I thought that the event celebrated a number of
clergy who were seeking justice. I could see how their agenda for
gays or blacks or women fit with my efforts in seeking justice for
Marlys, my wife's daughter who had been murdered. The parallels of
having to work with the political and legal systems, of persuading
people to take up our cause, of seeking having justice, gave me a
sense of solidarity with those at the event.

The service was very clearly about gays and lesbians, and the congregation did see a gay man in the pulpit. That was his topic, in contrast with Pastor Mary Albing. At LCCR, they don't see a lesbian but
instead see a pastor seeking to console those who are suffering. This
time the suffering was about the need gays have for justice.

Chapter 4

Why Should Jay Wiesner
Be a Pastor?

Jay Wiesner was born in New Ulm, Minnesota, a rural community south of the Twin Cities. Jay lived there until he went to college. "At five I knew I was different. I didn't feel right, but I had no clue. At puberty—when is that? Twelve or thirteen? I knew exactly who I was. But I wouldn't admit it to others, and I wouldn't admit it to myself. I prayed all the time for God to take it away."

From high school on, he dated girls, then women. From tenth grade to his second year of seminary he dated, and "never did I go more than three weeks between girlfriends because I didn't want people to know I am gay." He was engaged twice. The first time was not really serious. "We had been going steady and eventually said we probably should get married. The second engagement was more serious, but the marriage would have been tragic. I still see her, but her husband has issues with me being around."

Jay came out his second year at seminary. After coming out to a seminary professor, who would later give his ordination sermon, he thought, "I'm gay, I'm eating, therefore gay men eat." It seemed strange to him, and then he realized that he was finally putting his humanity and his sexuality together. He learned how to no longer be dehumanized. "I was on the cusp, coming out late in life, but kids are now coming out as teenagers."

Jay leads a program at Bethany to keep youth in the church. He has a camp. "Sure, gays coming out get shoved into their lockers at school, but more and more are accepted, even respected. It is important to deal with homosexuality when others of the same age are dealing with their own sexuality. This is the time to do it."

Hate Is The Sin

Jay started to wrestle with his vocation or call. "How do you serve God? Luther would argue that part of a call is to love your family, your children. So I asked, 'Who did God call me to be?' I struggled a long time to see what my call was for the church. I feel good about who I am in God's eyes. But who am I in the church?

"Homosexuality is not only about the sex act. It is a gender issue. Take note of how many rednecks don't mind lesbian porn but get suddenly violent about gay men."

Jay thinks that straight men can't say that another man is good-looking without being accused of being gay, but women can say, 'she's really good-looking.' Women can cross-dress but men can't.

"Straight men scare me," he added, looking at me without a smile. "Straight men represent danger."

Jay's work at Bethany has been as pastoral minister of outreach, which has included a lot of effort to reach the people in the Seward Neighborhood of Minneapolis where the church is located.

"Bethany," he says, "has many people who can only be part of this specific church. There are a number of people dealing with aspects of mental illness who worry about where they can go if not to Bethany. They may have issues with the congregation and leave, but they always come back because we welcome them. They come back because I am connected to them."

Jay believes that evangelism, the work he does, is a long and painful process. "To reach out to people who have not known Jesus is easier than getting people back who have been hurt by the church. Some people are haunted by something out of their past, and this means they believe they are not truly welcome in the church."

It takes a long time to build the trust, and then, sometimes, inadvertently even, all the old demons come back. These individuals know too well what the church is about.

"It is," he adds, "more important to look for the de-churched than the un-churched. It is so important for people to think, 'Maybe there is a place for me in the Lutheran Church.' Real healing is beautiful."

One of his goals is to keep children in the church. Cruel gay bashing attacks frustrate him. He says he wants every kid to be safe. He does criminal background checks on every volunteer, and never, ever is only one adult in contact with the kids. "We know how volatile this work is," he said.

Out of curiosity, I asked him if he believed in miracles where physical laws are changed or violated?

"I want to believe yes, but must admit I've never seen one. It is possible, I think. There are different gifts. I don't speak in tongues but have heard others do it. I have been brought closer to God through music. I remember an Amy Grant song about angels watching over me and thought it was terrible theology. I wondered if it meant that angels weren't watching over others. Why me and not you?"

I said, "It goes back to the old argument in Job. If you do good, God will bless you and if you do bad, God will punish you."

"That is utter nonsense," he replied. We agreed on that.

At the end of our conversation, Jay talked about being called into ministry. "I am called to be a pastor and people tell me that. In discerning a call, there is not only the inner call but the community also has to acknowledge a call for a person."

His struggle with a call is internal and external. At Bethany, he is affirmed in both aspects.

AN EXTRAORDINARY ORDINATION

A month later I received an invitation to attend an ordination ceremony at which Jay Wiesner would take part in what is called an "extraordinary ordination." The Extraordinary Candidacy Project began in 1993, as a response to the ELCA's policy on not ordaining or calling otherwise qualified candidates if they were in an open, committed, same-gender relationship. The ELCA considers these "out" gays and lesbians in violation of, or unable to sign, the "Visions and Expectations" statement.

Bethany Lutheran Church on East Franklin ordained Jay Wiesner on Sunday, July 25, 2004, in a service held at Plymouth Congregational Church. That church was chosen because it had a sanctuary large enough for the great number of people expected to attend.

When I arrived at Plymouth Church, I had to park in an overflow parking lot. The sanctuary was almost totally full, and I found an open pew on the side aisle. Someone would later say that they counted over a thousand persons in attendance.

The ordination service itself was high church and a lot of fun. I would later describe it to the Minneapolis Area Synod Council as "really religious."

The sermon by Rev. Dr. Gwen Sayler made a great analogy between the way Jesus was received in his days and the way the church has received Jay. She had served as Jay's Hebrew Bible professor at Wartburg Seminary and knew her biblical texts well. She talked about Jesus first. Citing John 7: 37-52, Dr. Sayler asked, "What to do with his invitation to drink from him, his promise that from the believer's heart will flow rivers of living water? What do we do with a guy who sounds like the real thing but comes from the wrong place?"

Dr. Sayler went through other examples of water in the New Testament, of John baptizing Jesus to the water flowing from Jesus' side at his crucifixion. She talked about rivers, and then Dr. Sayler spoke directly to Jay.

"Jay Alan Wiesner, baptized in and nourished by the living water, by the call of Bethany Lutheran Church you come before us today for ordination into the ministry of word and sacrament."

She affirmed him and his qualifications, then acknowledged the stress Bethany faced. "To state the obvious, our celebration here today is a cause of controversy for many in the church that we love. To those who are confused about or challenge the validity of the ordination we celebrate today, I issue an invitation—come to Bethany Lutheran Church and see. Come, witness the ministries happening there. Participate in worship, hear the preaching and teaching, observe the outreach and pastoral care. Come and see. Who knows—you may hear the Spirit wind blowing and the water flowing free."

The ordination took place in the center of the main aisle, with hundreds of supportive Lutherans crowding around Jay. Bethany Lutheran's Senior Pastor Steve Benson ordained Jay and retired ELCA bishops Paul Egertson and Lowell Erdahl assisted.

Later that evening, my wife, Fran, and I joined Pastor Mary Albing and her partner, Jane Lien, at a party celebrating Jay's ordination. The room was filled with joy and laughter as Jay's many supporters rejoiced. Others who also needed to overcome what they saw as injustice took heart that because Jay had made the step, others could as well. Only later would they need to think about what the Minneapolis Area Synod Council and Bishop Craig Johnson would do about the ordination. But that would not come until after Bethany Lutheran

Church installed Jay as its associate pastor. That installation took place on August 1, 2004, at 9:30 a.m. at Bethany Lutheran Church. The Synod Council would not meet until September 9.

FOLLOWING THEIR CONSCIENCES

The Minneapolis Area Synod Council meets about six times a year. The Synod is the ELCA's largest, with over 170 congregations. These churches are grouped in conferences. In 2003, I was elected to the Council from the Northern Conference, which had eleven churches including my home church, Long Lake Lutheran in rural Isanti County. Jay Wiesner represented the conference that included Bethany Lutheran Church.

The Synod Council meetings are held in a first-floor conference room in the Minnesota Church Center on West Franklin Avenue in Minneapolis. The Synod offices on the sixth floor do not have a room large enough for these meetings. Tables are set up in a large, rectangular arrangement so that we face to the middle and can see all the council members and guests.

Bishop Craig E. Johnson has been the Bishop of the Minneapolis Area Synod since his election and installation in October 2001. Ms. Kari Christianson is the vice president of the synod and chair of the Synod Council. Karen Jenkins, now deceased, was the Council Secretary and Bud Meadley is the Treasurer. Also on the council are nine pastors and nine laypersons. Three from each group represent "tables" or committees that also carry out the work of the Synod. Six pastors and six laypersons represent these tables.

Bishop Johnson and the other officers sat along the tables that were to the left of the doors. I sat at the other end, facing the Bishop. Persons from Bethany Lutheran Church in Minneapolis were visiting at this meeting to discuss their action of ordaining and calling Jay Wiesner. They sat along the long wall opposite the doors to the room and behind Jay. At the appropriate place on the agenda, we began a conversation with the visitors.

A woman identified herself as Lynn, and said she spoke as the Bethany Lutheran Church Council President. She thanked us for allowing her group to speak to the Synod Council. Lynn said that four to five years ago, the members began to discern the future of Bethany

Lutheran Church. It is an inner-city church, with many immigrants in the neighborhood. They decided to open the door and welcome GLBT people, among others. They focused on the de-churched rather than the un-churched. They hired Jay as a pastoral outreach minister, and, over time, saw God's call to him to be a pastor. Eventually they followed their conscience to call and ordain Jay, and the vote was nearly unanimous.

One of the pastors on the Council asked if the congregation thought about the consequences of calling Jay, and Lynn replied that they talked at length about all the consequences, including risk to the present pastor, Steve Benson, and financial issues.

Another woman who identified herself as a long-time member said they had Bible studies and prayer, and the decision wasn't made when Jay arrived. It took years. She said, "I don't want to meet my maker if I denied Jay's call."

Someone else said that they also considered the consequences if they didn't call Jay.

A pastor on the Council asked the visitors why they didn't wait until the Churchwide Assembly in 2005, and Lynn replied that they lacked faith in the system. "In 2003, they put off the vote."

Bishop Johnson said that he had met with the church council, and that "people of passion" spoke with him. He also acknowledged that they were asking themselves what it meant to disobey the church they love. Bishop Johnson then asked, "Should the ELCA throw out five-hundred years of polity and have congregations ordain whomever they wish?"

Bethany Pastor Steve Benson replied, "The bishop should ordain, except in extraordinary circumstances."

Bishop Johnson said, "Steve and Jay have shown respect."

Someone said, "One can't do civil disobedience without taking the consequences."

A layperson from the Council pointed out that by ordaining Jay, Bethany had made it difficult for the bishop. "The only thing preventing Jay's ordination is that he is in a committed relationship. But that is significant."

After complimenting Jay on his work in outreach for Bethany, a pastor asked, "What led the congregation to ordain to Word and Sacrament rather than keeping on with his present good work?"

Several women replied that the congregation had developed a relationship with Jay and wanted to extend his contribution. "We don't want two classes of Christians."

After a few more minutes of conversation, the group from Bethany Lutheran Church left the Council meeting. We talked amongst ourselves about what could and should be done. One of Bishop Johnson's staff outlined the options as set out in the church constitution and governance rules.

Some time later, Bishop Johnson issued a censure and admonition to Bethany Lutheran Church. The letter indicated that Bishop Johnson made his decision after much prayer and listening. However, he felt he had to send the letter because the congregation had violated its covenant with the ELCA by calling someone not on the ELCA clergy roster. His letter said, "Bethany Lutheran Church after debate, discussion and vote willfully disregarded this critical accord of congregational life in the ELCA."

Chapter 5

Aftermath of Refusal

On a bright, sunny Sunday in November I attended a worship service at Bethany Lutheran Church. This church began in controversy in 1902, when a pastor at Trinity Lutheran Church was accused of "improper conduct" while on a trip to Norway. Although the charges were never substantiated, the pastor resigned. Some of the Trinity members believed in that pastor, however, and formed a new church, Bethany Lutheran, with him as its pastor. He served until 1911 and was active in the community, even serving as president of the Minneapolis Board of Education.

This particular Sunday, Senior Pastor Steve Benson preached the sermon. Steve has been at Bethany since 1995. He has completed graduate work in Christian-Muslim relations, has strong experience in global mission issues, and came to Bethany, in part, because of the number of Muslim refugees in the Seward neighborhood around Bethany. Steve's sermon focused on conflict in the world and a need for God's peace.

Jay Wiesner served as the Liturgist at the service. I watched him lead the congregation through the invocation, prayers, and other parts of the service. I had been a seminarian once, in addition to my theological studies, and I learned what the church (in various denominations) believes about Word and Sacrament. Independent of the joy I saw as Jay performed the words of institution, I felt required by what I believe to accept his ordination, or my acceptance of the bread and wine would be a sin of disrespect of the body and blood of Jesus. The church teaches that Christ's body and blood are (depending on the particular denomination) present in some way in the Eucharist. Under normal circumstances, presiding over the sacrament is restricted to those whose ordination has been called by the church. I admit I struggled with what Jay did that morning.

Hate Is The Sin

What is it like to look into the eyes of a person as he gives you the bread and says, "This is the body of Christ, broken and given for you," when you know that your bishop has refused to ordain him? Initially I felt troubled by the fact that Jay performed the sacramental transformation of bread and wine into the body and blood of Christ, and yet, somehow, it was right.

As I walked up the aisle to stand before Jay, I had some serious thoughts. I attended his ordination—an extraordinary ordination. Now my decision to take communion appeared to be taking a side in the debate. The issue isn't whether he hands me the bread or I receive it from Pastor Steve Benson, who the ELCA ordained. In most ELCA churches, laypersons and clergy together dispense the elements to the congregation. I do it myself at my home church, after Pastor Howard has said the words of institution.

My concern arose because Jay, rather than Steve, said the words of institution. It is one thing to argue that Pastor Mary Albing was ordained within the rules of the ELCA, and quite another to accept Jay's Extraordinary Candidate Project ordination. But who really decides that an ordination is essential to confer on an individual the ability to consecrate bread and wine into the Body of Christ?

What about those in the pews who aren't theologically trained? Or who aren't aware of Jay's ordination situation? What about strangers? What about visiting clergy? Is Bethany fair to decide that the extraordinary ordination is valid even though they admit it is ecclesiastical disobedience? Is it consistent with the decision of the bishop because he didn't shut them down? Can I let Bishop Johnson take the rap? Is it right? Loving? Christian? What would Jesus do? Mere mortals like me will be asked to debate this issue of ordination of people like Jay in Orlando. Is that different? Yes.

I looked into Jay's eyes as he gave me the consecrated bread. "The body of Christ, broken for you," he said. "Amen," I replied.

AN INWARDLY DIRECTED NORWEGIAN CLUB

A few weeks later, I met Senior Pastor Steve Benson at a coffee shop. No more than average height, Steve has gray-streaked hair and a mostly gray beard. His handshake was firm.

Steve grew up as a member of the Lutheran Church-Missouri Synod and eventually went to seminary. He hated the split over closed communion and woman's ordination, and ended up in the ELCA. He says he also reacted against the liberal sentiment of making decisions about what feels nice, adding that not being concerned about what is right and wrong is repulsive too. He favors slow, deliberate, respectful debate before making changes.

When Bethany started to look for a pastor, it was divided. The call committee had three who wanted to keep traditions and three who wanted change, and they all had to agree. Sides were divided over generational lines. Some said, "We always did it this way" and others said, "It isn't working." They looked at seven candidates and liked none. They looked at another five, and Steve became the one the committee agreed on. "The call committee," Steve said, "was reluctant and functioned slowly, deliberately, and respectfully."

We talked very little about Jay, other than a few comments on Bishop Johnson's letter. Steve said he didn't want to be too critical of the letter.

"I want to do what is in the best interest of the church. It doesn't make sense to argue about things. Having said that, there are certain issues. First, we did not 'preempt' the ELCA process. I would like a different word. Second, we are not substituting a church for the synod. We did change our constitution and that was not accepted by the synod council. Third, saying the ordination caused stress with the Oromo Lutheran Church (which was sharing the Bethany facility and whose members are recent immigrants from the horn of Africa) isn't really true."

Steve said that they had mature Christian conversations when Bethany became a Reconciling In Christ congregation. I took mature to mean they respected the various choices even though they weren't in agreement.

Early on, Steve explained, Bethany was an inwardly directed Norwegian club and the pastor served as the chaplain of the club. In the early 1900s, the church housed sociopolitical activists for labor, progressive, populist politics. The neighborhood now has 10 to 20 percent ethnic minority. Two days after 9/11, Bethany posted a notice of its sanctuary as a safe place for Muslims in the community to be without fear. Steve is proud when he says they are seeking a dialogue with Muslims, "not diluting Christianity," he cautions, but hoping to form a positive relationship with them. He sees common commitment from respectful dialogue.

After the congregation began to decline in membership because of the neighborhood change, the remnant saw a need to connect with the diversity of the people who had moved into the neighborhood. A pastor came for two years, left as a failed call, and then the church had an interim for another two years.

In December 1995, Steve took the call and saw a vision for the church.

As he explained, "It was two or three years before sexuality became an issue. At first there were racial, cultural, ethnic, age, physical and mental handicap issues for people, all of whom experience discrimination for things about themselves they can't change. So too with sexuality."

Steve told me how Bethany had become isolated from the neighborhood—seen as a fortress on the corner. He said it had to change, and it now has a reputation of being a valued neighborhood partner. Steve's wife is on a neighborhood group board and sometimes it has meetings at the church. They had a memorial service for lymphoma victims.

"The neighborhood is committed to human values, some in the church and some who reject the idea of church but are beginning to see Bethany as a partner in values."

I asked if the church was concerned about financial survival because of the small number of members and especially after deciding to call Jay. Bethany received some money from a foundation and from a program designed to help places like Bethany known as "In The City For Good." I also learned that Steve works part time as chaplain at a local nursing home and Jay works at Augsburg College. These paychecks go to the church to support them.

Steve talked about his theology. "Lutheran Scriptural tradition is to interpret the Bible in so far as it points us to Christ, and the gospel of Christ is the key—the lens through which we interpret all. When I hear people make the arguments and attitudes for exclusion, I can't distinguish between them and the Pharisees of Jesus' day. But I'm trying to avoid polarization. I try to have our church follow Jesus' example of love without diluting the gospel. Christ went to the cross rather than exclude the excluded. We are not trying to impose our agenda on the larger church. But take a look at us."

I mentioned that I had enjoyed his sermon and agreed with his position on wars. I also said I understood what he meant about the congregation and its diversity.

"I've seen it. My previous call was in India. When I came here I wanted a ministry to bridge divisions in the human community and help people see Christ's ministry of reconciliation. Prejudice reduction is what I try to do. What is the congregation doing, and where is God calling them to go? Can we discern and develop a focus and direction to facilitate and empower—to follow through? My job is to give them courage to act on what they discern as God's calling."

This led me to mention Jay's statement about internal and external calls. "Jay has told me about his feelings of call and of the affirmation he has received from others."

"I agree that Jay had both. It's obvious." Steve laughed. "Someone said that some members left the church over Jay's ordination, but it wasn't true. They said 'Well didn't so and so leave?' I said, 'No he's sitting right over there.' The truth is some have left over politics, but not over sexuality. You don't have to soft-peddle what you believe to avoid hurting others, but you must show respect for those who disagree. Someone asked me, 'If I can't accept GLBT people, does that mean I can't stay at Bethany?' I said they should stay and that family did—they even helped with Jay's ordination."

Our time was just about finished when Steve said he had to tell me one story of someone who came to Bethany not long after 9/11.

"A Pakistani man married a Christian woman. He once attended her church, because Muslims and Christians have some things in common, and as he left, the pastor at the door welcomed him. Then, apparently deciding this was his only chance, the pastor said 'You must accept Jesus Christ as your personal savior or you will go to hell.' It took the Pakistani ten years to enter a church again, and that was Bethany, for a forum on getting to know the Muslim neighbors."

WE WANT TO BE AN ACCEPTING CHURCH

I went back to Bethany on another Sunday, worshiped with the congregation, and walked up to the altar to again receive communion consecrated by Pastor Jay Wiesner. After the service some of those who had come to the synod council met me in the library. Our conversation was to be the adult Sunday school session.

I sat at one end of a large table and the others gathered around the table. Jay, who sat on a stuffed easy chair to my right, introduced me, saying that I had been a member of the synod council when they presented their case, and that I was writing a book about the issues of human sexuality in the ELCA.

The current council president said, "I was on the team that hired Jay and called him to ordination. We have been very busy as a congregation. Look at where we're going. I see a lot of new faces, and we have an increase in membership. But we are facing financial battles. We focus on evangelism."

"That's right," an older woman said. "We are called to be a light to the world and encourage church leadership."

The memory of the first time I took communion from Jay came back, and I repeated it to the group. I admitted I felt some concern about his consecration as one ordained by the Extraordinary Candidacy Project.

Jay lit up with a big smile. "It is always on my mind that people might not come up."

"It is refreshing," the council president said. "This is the real Jesus. There's so much hypocrisy and finger-pointing in the ELCA. We have gone against church policy, but we met the congregation where they are. They know what it is like to be cast out."

As he spoke a little girl, maybe six or seven, sat on a bench near Jay, listening.

The middle-aged woman spoke up again. "We didn't intend to be a gay church. We want to reach all those who are outside the church. We're here for the community." She looked around the room seeking approval.

A thin woman in her fifties said, "I joined this church, and my boss is a strong Methodist. He said, 'You've been married and widowed twice. Why are you in a homosexual church?' Of course others see what they want to see."

An older woman sitting on my left said, "I joined because my son is a pastor. He is always for the outcasts."

"You were Missouri Synod Lutherans?" I asked.

"Yes," she said, nodding for emphasis. "Well, we had some problems with that church. We were in the Missouri Synod because my husband said we should go where our parents went to church. So we did. But we didn't like a lot of their beliefs. We read and studied and learned." She waved her hand as if to dismiss the past. "But this was what my son wanted, so we told him to go for it. I remember when the council asked, 'Why can't we ordain Jay?' He said, 'We can.'"

A tall man introduced himself. "Evangelism is strong at Bethany. In our pastor we have good leadership that we trust. He points us in a direction, and then I learn what I am doing. We had many group discussions and I know God is moving us in this direction."

Another woman spoke. "I've been a member for twenty years. We had a previous pastor who didn't focus on sexuality. Who did? We didn't know we had a gay choir member, but he opened our eyes to how gays are suffering when he came out to us. Ten years later two men came and taught Sunday school. They are partnered. One of them is now a United Church of Christ pastor, but both men were role models for us."

A young woman raised her hand. "I went to the synod council meeting too. I didn't speak, but I had to be there. Nothing was more important. It was a question of justice. Gays aren't lesser than other parts of creation. I'm weak and fearful. It starts with young kids putting people down with insults. Like calling each other 'faggot.' People can't be who they aren't."

The council president spoke again, as if for the congregation. "The reason Jay was brought to Bethany was to have someone find disenfranchised people. He was minister of outreach. In drafting our mission statement, we want to be Reconciling In Christ, but we are not a gay church. We want to be an accepting church and use outreach to be involved in so much more. It isn't a question of mental illness for one member or being gay for another or whatever. We had almost unanimous acceptance of Jay—and our goal is to be accepting of all persons—no matter what their circumstances."

One of the older women reminded us that, "Two people from here at Bethany are UCC pastors, including one who is gay. Our congregation talked at great length and we come to God's table even when we don't agree. It is wonderful to watch. We don't agree but feel comfortable with one another, and we try to be sure we don't make others uncomfortable."

Jay spoke up. "I did a marriage and the couple insisted that I tell the congregation that I am gay. We want this to be a safe place."

"Some members voted not to let Jay in," the president said, "and we lost some people before Jay came. Funny though, some who voted not to hire Jay then asked, 'Why isn't Jay ordained?'"

A woman smiled knowingly. "I was raised in the Assembly of God Church. Then my brother-in-law came out and I changed my views on homosexuality."

The council president agreed. "Jesus fought against hypocrisy. Here in the ELCA it is okay to be a gay pastor as long as you don't love someone. I want to fight against that hypocrisy."

"There are five or ten gay pastors in the ELCA who are out," Jay said, "and hundreds who are not. It is literally hell struggling with serving or not serving, and we have twenty-four hundred pastoral vacancies. Maybe God is sending us gays who are qualified to work? It only took me five years. Thank God I've been on the top of the list."

"One pastor was selected by our conference to be at the Churchwide Assembly because of his leadership," someone said. "He understands political red tape, and Bethany is proud of his leadership. He had a mandate at the conference. We try to do things as a community."

Then the time was up. Jay and the council president thanked me for having an interest in their church and their struggles. I told them I appreciated their time and the conversation.

Chapter 6

Journey Together Faithfully

The ELCA struggled with issues of human sexuality for many years before the merger in 1987 that formed the largest Lutheran denomination in the United States. Individual churches such as Lutheran Church of Christ the Redeemer, which began its first study in 1975, raised issues that church leaders recognized as troubling to many congregations.

Other churches simply condemned homosexuality, and in some cases homosexuals. The divisiveness caused by various readings of biblical texts to prove or disprove what was a sin and what was not, eventually led to formal, denomination-wide studies, with the hope of finding a way for a better understanding of human sexuality for Lutherans.

In 2001, the ELCA Churchwide Assembly mandated that the church conduct two studies on human sexuality. The first, a study of whether or not persons in same-gender relationships could have their unions blessed and could be considered for service as pastors of an ELCA congregation, would be presented as recommendations for consideration at a future Churchwide Assembly. It was brought to the 2005 Churchwide Assembly in Orlando, Florida. The ELCA chartered a second study to arrive at a general social statement on human sexuality, now scheduled to be brought to the 2009 Churchwide Assembly to be held in Minneapolis.

The ELCA Church Council commissioned the preparation and dissemination of a study guide for use by those congregations and individuals who chose to be involved in the process. This includes an opportunity to submit comments and reflections to the Task Force for ELCA Studies on Sexuality, which conducts the studies. A first guide, titled *Journey Together Faithfully: ELCA Studies on Sexuality: Part One* was published as a sixteen-page booklet by the denomination in 2002, and dealt with "common convictions" that the Task Force believed were accepted by most ELCA parishioners.

In the fall of 2002, Long Lake Lutheran Church in Isanti, Minnesota, had several sessions on the Part One study guide. Members of the congregation requested the action, saying that "Long Lake Lutheran is doing nothing about the ELCA study." Senior Pastor Howard Skulstad led the group and limited the conversations to the issues in the Part One guide.

The four topics, God's Creation and New Creation, Single Adults, Responsible Procreation and Parenting, and Some Misuses of Sexuality, did not address same-gender activity of any kind. Pastor Skulstad was firm that those activities would be covered when Part Two arrived.

In September 2003, the ELCA published a second booklet of forty-nine pages titled *Journey Together Faithfully: The Church and Homosexuality Study Guide: Part Two,* in which it asked "members of the ELCA to consider how this church should respond to the requests to bless same-sex unions and to ordain, consecrate, or commission people in committed same-sex unions."

Also in September 2003, the ELCA released a twenty-four page background booklet titled *Background Essay of Biblical Texts for Use with Part Two.* Rev. Dr. James M. Childs, Director for the ELCA Studies on Sexuality, wrote the introduction. The authors of the paper, Rev. Dr. Arland J. Hultgren of Luther Seminary in St. Paul, Minnesota, and Rev. Dr. Walter F. Taylor of Trinity Lutheran Seminary in Columbus, Ohio, were praised by Dr. Childs as "both among the most highly respected biblical scholars in the ELCA" (p. 1). Childs said that the paper provided "an excellent account of how scholars have interpreted the texts that deal most directly with same-sex activity" (p. 1). The paper deals with specific texts and phrases, but notes, "Actually the entire biblical witness has to be borne in mind, for no one passage or cluster of passages should be studied in isolation" (p. 3). In the study sessions I attended, too many people read a text in isolation, out of context, and literally.

MY READING OF THE BIBLE

Part of theological reflection on issues involves being engaged with the words of the Bible. I believe the human sexuality debate is both secular and Christian in nature. It is secular because liberals and conservatives debate these issues, just as they did with the right of women to vote or the legitimacy of separate-but-equal schools for racially different peoples. A caution: I am not equating human sexuality issues with suffrage for women or civil rights for minorities because those analogies don't address the real issues. The common thread, however, is that these were debated in Congress, in the courts, in newspapers, on school boards, and everywhere in society. Laws and amendments to state and federal constitutions were political issues that found voters divided.

They are also debated in the church. Scripture was and is used to support one position or another. Professors Hultgren and Taylor caution against "proof-texting," where both sides cite texts in the Bible and argue that the passages should be interpreted the way they see them. But reading the Bible is not done in a vacuum, nor is interpretation a simple matter that all can agree upon. Before I look at various positions on certain texts, it may be of value to describe how I read the Scriptures, or, at least, how I think I read them.

In 1983, less than four years after my wife's daughter, Marlys, had been murdered, I became much more active in the local church—at my wife's insistence. I started reading the Bible and joined a Bible study group at the church. I had been raised as a Roman Catholic, but had left the church in my twenties. Still, I knew some of the gospel stories from what was read at mass. When I began to read the Bible in depth and tried to figure out what was being said, I marveled at the adventures of Abraham and Moses and David in the Old Testament and paid more attention to what Jesus said in the gospels. One day we were studying chapter six of the Gospel according to St. John, where Jesus is telling his disciples about his body and blood being the source of eternal life. When I got to verse 66, I read:

> Because of this many of his disciples turned back and no longer went about with him. So Jesus asked the twelve, "Do you also wish to go away?" Simon Peter answered him, "Lord, to whom can we go? You have the words of eternal life. We have come to believe and know that you are the Holy One of God."

That reading startled me. Peter sounds almost irreverent when he asks Jesus where else he could go to find eternal life. My actual thought at the time was that Peter was being sarcastic, like "Well, duh! Where else can we go? No one else does miracles, and one of these days you will probably walk on water." The truth of his question struck me with such force that nearly a quarter of a century later, I still remember the power of these words. Where else could I go? To whom can I go?

This was also my first awareness that reading the Bible is done in context, as I would later learn in seminary. That day I was reading the Bible as an angry man whose stepdaughter had been murdered, and since I didn't know who to be angry at, I saw Peter as being sarcastic to Jesus. I would have read it differently before Marlys' murder, and I read it differently today. When we read the Bible, for any reason, we have to remember our own personal context. We also have to be tolerant of others who find different meanings when they seek answers. And, since there was no where else for me to go, by fall of that year, I was enrolled in seminary.

Through the years since I first began to study the Bible, read theology, and think about God in the world, I have changed my mind about many things. God's role in the death of a young person is one issue. It took a while, but I realize now that God didn't take Marlys' life, the serial killer who murdered her did. I personally don't see God acting directly in this world, but I do see God acting through people who seek to do God's will. In other words, I don't believe in miracles but I do see miraculous things happen. I am quite aware that others may see God's action in the world to be different from or even opposite to my understanding.

On human sexuality issues, many opposed to gay ordination and unions say that a new way to read the Bible needs to be shown as having merit before they will change their minds. Advocates for these changes in the church say that it has already been done. There is a third option, I believe, that allows for individuals to follow their conscience, reading the text within their own context. But there is a catch to this option. In 2004, Bishop Craig Johnson of the Minneapolis Area Synod said, "There is a new model, of seeing two different biblical views as biblically legitimate but not convergent, as it applies to sexual issues." The catch is that we have to admit that the other person's biblical views are legitimate.

Genesis 1:27 says, "So God created humankind in his image, in the image of God he created them; male and female he created them."

Genesis 2:24-25 says, "Therefore a man leaves his father and his mother and clings to his wife, and they become one flesh. And the man and his wife were both naked, and were not ashamed."

These two texts are used as support for God only intending heterosexual orientation. But when a gay person reads Genesis 1:27, he might say, "In spite of the hate I have encountered for being gay, this text says that God created me in God's image. And it says God created my partner in God's image." When reading Genesis 2:24-25, he says, "I have left my mother and father and I cling to my partner, because just as straight people are created by God and are attracted to opposite-sex persons, I and my partner are created by God and are attracted to same-sex persons. Otherwise, God did not make me what I am."

The point here is not to claim as absolute that gays and lesbians are so oriented because God created them that way; though most gays and lesbians I've talked with believe their orientation comes from within, as if they were created that way. Most say that they never chose to be gay any more than straight people choose to be straight. Many have admitted to fighting their feelings and praying to God to be changed.

My point is that gays and lesbians have as much right to read the Bible in their own context as anyone else in the church. When people at LCCR read these texts, they see their biblical views as biblically legitimate, and so do the people at Long Lake Lutheran. The views might be opposite, but the tensions won't be released until each sees the other's views as legitimate and not as plain wrong.

Pastor Mary Albing says this is a time when the church is trying to have discernment. She believes the conversation must be broadened into more than a debate about biblical interpretation. Mary often says, "My congregation does not see me as a lesbian in the pulpit, but they do see a pastor seeking to console those who are suffering."

THE TASK FORCE ISSUES A REPORT

On January 13, 2005, the ELCA issued an "embargoed" edition of the *Report and Recommendations from the Task Force for Evangelical Lutheran Church in America Studies on Sexuality.* The ELCA distributed the report to all rostered clergy, giving them a one-day advance look at the text which would not be available to the general public until January 14.

I found the recommendations to be less than prophetic. They included: (1) concentrate on finding ways to live together faithfully in the midst of our disagreements, (2) continue to provide pastoral care to all, but marriage is still between man and woman, and (3) if a partnered gay minister is otherwise qualified and is called, don't discipline them or the church if they are called.

I was disappointed that the task force didn't take a stand, one way or the other, on the propriety of pastors blessing same-gender commitment unions. I understood the unwillingness to address the issue of "marriage" between persons of the same gender because it is a secular issue. Even in church weddings, the couple is married "by the power of the State of Minnesota" or other jurisdiction where the marriage takes place. A wedding is really an event conducted under the power of the state to grant a marriage license and the clergy person is functioning as an officer of the state. This legal event also takes on a sacramental importance where couples eagerly seek God's blessings and the affirmation of their union to each other and by the congregation.

I wished the report had more explicitly stated that it is a legitimate understanding of ELCA polity to permit those pastors who believe their pastoral duties include caring for gay couples to affirm their commitment in a church setting. Then I recalled Pastor Don Luther's conversation with his bishop when he decided to perform such a ceremony. "If it walks like a duck, and quacks like a duck. . ." Church blessings do look like weddings.

I was interested in the reactions of others. Because I was in Florida, I couldn't attend the Minneapolis Area Synod pastor's meeting to discuss and react to the report. But there are Lutherans in Florida too, and I located one ELCA church that had a discussion group planned.

I visited the ELCA Lutheran Church in southern Florida. The pastor met me when I entered the Masonic Lodge building they are using for a temporary church while their first sanctuary is completed.

We were joined by a retired ELCA pastor from suburban Pittsburgh and his wife. A widow of a pastor from near Rockford, Illinois, also came to the church. A couple from Melrose, Minnesota, a man from Bloomington, Minnesota, a woman from Ohio, and another couple also joined the group. Eleven of us gathered to talk about human sexuality.

When we introduced ourselves, the retired pastor said that he was from Pittsburgh and a Steelers fan, pronouncing it 'still-ers'—saying that was how natives said the team's name.

I said it might be nice if they got to play the Philadelphia Eagles in the Super Bowl, as both Pennsylvania teams were still in the play-offs.

He replied, "I hate the Eagles. I never want them to win."

I wondered how we could talk about blessing same-sex unions and ordaining such people if this mind-set was prevalent. My prior conversations at other churches had shown a lot of hate, even with the caveat that we love the sinner.

The pastor opened with a reading from Romans 14, which focused on not passing judgment on others. He said, "Paul had to deal with food, both with kosher and with food previously offered to idols and false gods." He asked us to list other issues and most of us spoke up.

The retired pastor said that just meeting in a Masonic lodge is amazing since Masons used to be prohibited by Lutherans, and then it became okay for lay people but not clergy, and now no one cares. The document that pastors sign, called "Visions and Expectations" outlines the rules of conduct for those called into ministry in the ELCA. Thirty years ago, those rules prohibited membership in "secret" societies such as the Masons.

The presiding pastor asked, "Why is it so hard to include people on both sides? What has the church failed to do over the past thirty to fifty years? There are two kinds of people. Some people are wired to be duty bound and live out the rules. Others, consequentalists, see it is okay to break the rules because of the consequences."

He seemed to be struggling and I wondered if he saw the consequences that gays and lesbians experience in the church. I also understood what he meant by rules, that they are to be more than what is written in "Visions and Expectations."

The woman from Melrose said that her church just called a woman as the pastor for the first time and it was a major step. Looking at biblical exegesis, she felt that St. Paul was time-bound. Now the challenge is over sexuality. She added that the choir director of her church is a lesbian in a long-term relationship but does not flaunt it to the congregation.

The retired pastor said he has a problem because homosexuality is not normal. "I can't understand why a classmate came out of the closet after twenty years of ministry. He lost his job even though he has never been in a same-sex relationship. The congregation just didn't want him."

Someone asked if it made a difference if sexuality was genetic? The man from Melrose asked, "If it is genetic or if it is a choice, does it make a difference? In either case, it's what the Bible says, if that is our authority." He wanted to interpret homosexual acts as they were in Paul's time, when they didn't have a concept of a loving, same-gender relationship.

His wife suggested that small groups are a way to get to know people and overcome bias.

The moderating pastor said, "His own children accept gays more so than racial or cultural differences." From his expression I could see that this troubled him, and, perhaps, he felt more open to accepting those racial differences.

We had a very long discussion on the use of statistics in the report. "They aren't valid according to statistical standards," said an accountant who admitted he is not a statistics expert.

The pastor brought us back to the topic. "We're getting into a bind. How do we talk about sin in the world?" He wanted homosexuality to be outside the created order, outside boundaries. He would not bless same-sex unions but would tell them why and would work with them. "A prophetic voice is what we need," he added.

Someone said GLBT advocates are forcing the issue, telling the church how they want to be treated.

The pastor said that he has a gene that wants him to be 600 pounds, "I have to work on restricting the amount of food I eat."

Near the end of the session, the retired pastor told of singing in a choir while standing between two homosexuals who are integrated into the congregation. "Being involved with 'those people' softens the fears," he said, "but I would say no to blessing their union or ordaining them."

The report of the Task Force had not changed the minds of any of these people, but it did bring them together to talk to each other in a respectful way. That, for me, was a good accomplishment.

Chapter 7

Dissatisfaction

While still in Florida, I sought the opinion of someone who had experienced another denomination's debate on human sexuality. The Reverend Donald A. Fishburne, DMin, is the rector at St. Michael and All the Angels Episcopal Church on Sanibel Island. We met in his office. Of average build, balding, and with a compassionate smile, he often breaks into a grin when he hears something he likes. He wore khaki pants and a matching sport shirt, casual boating shoes and no socks. We sat in two wooden chairs separated partly by an end table with a lamp.

Donald grew up in the Episcopal Church in the south, then went to seminary in Alexandria, Virginia. That was about the time his denomination began ordaining women. He had a ministry in the Southeastern United States for twenty-five years before coming to Sanibel Island.

When I asked about hate, he said he sees people who are indignant at homosexual behavior. Plus, they have a fear, he added. Upon reflection he agreed that he had seen hate as I described it. However, he added, many people in the Episcopal Church are aware of the homosexual issues, but it is simply not discussed. I thought of 'don't ask, don't tell' situations.

Donald has not had much practical experience with homosexuality in a church. In his first call at a small parish, he didn't think he had any gay parishioners. He next went to the staff at St. Michael Charleston (South Carolina—founded in 1750), which was a very artistic community where gays and straight people lived in tolerance. Then, he went to Christ Church in Charlotte, North Carolina, where 5 percent of the people were gay. He dislikes those who are intentionally intolerant of others for any reason, and particularly those who are militantly so. Then he went to Augusta, Georgia, in the old south. In

Hate Is The Sin

the decade of the '90s, when gays started coming out, it became less possible to politely ignore them. Because the atmosphere is more open, fear and anxiety have taken hold.

"Here at St. Michael and All the Angels," he said, sounding grateful, "fewer than a dozen people are militantly, fiercely intolerant, and there are, perhaps, at least that many in long-term relationships who don't hide what they are but aren't intolerant and don't call attention to themselves. I get angry with people who make a fuss and gay couples at this church aren't making an issue out of sexuality. There are two things about Sanibel," he added. "People are here because they want to be, and because they can afford it. They've had vocations, careers, done important things, and see sexuality as no big deal."

He went to the Episcopal Church USA General Convention at Minneapolis in 2003 as an observer, paying his own way. Donald wanted to go to Minneapolis to see if people were being faithful, and he saw that they prayed and worshiped and had thoughtful, intelligent views, both liberal and conservative. "I had no vote but if I did, I would have voted against Bishop Robinson's election. If I had said that in the pulpit, my Associate Rector Suzi Post would have said, 'I didn't go but I would have voted for him.' But that's just a hypothetical situation. I have bigger problems than sexuality. In my twenty-fifth anniversary sermon, I said that the greater sin is not sexuality or greed or lust, but mean-spirited gossip. This is the nastiest sin I see. The Episcopal Church says we speak in truth and love, and a lot of folks don't do that."

He works with a group known as Via Media, or middle way, which is a grassroots-styled organization seeking to heal things that divide Christians. He gave me their brochure. I like this statement:

> O God of truth and peace, who raised up your servant Richard Hooker (a 16th century English theologian) in a day of bitter controversy to defend with sound reasoning and great charity the catholic and reformed religion: Grant that we may maintain the middle way, not as a compromise for the sake of peace, but as a comprehension for the sake of truth; through Jesus Christ our Lord, who lives and reigns with you and the Holy Spirit, one God, for ever and ever. Amen.

After the convention, his bishop, John Lipscomb, Bishop of Southwest Florida, was surprised by two things. The first was that the majority of the clergy (and some lay people) under him were not as conservative as he thought. Secondly, too many self-identified conservatives have been mean to him. Even though Bishop Lipscomb is a moderate, or a conservative who speaks with moderates, and even though he did vote against approving Robinson's election, he has been hurt by mean-spirited responses condemning him for not being forceful enough against the Bishop Robinson matter.

When the presiding bishop came to see the damage from Hurricane Charlie on Sanibel and Captiva Islands, someone asked him about gay ordination.

Donald was frustrated by people ignoring the devastation. "Human sexuality can be such a distraction. In the 1960s, "the presiding bishop asked, 'Why do we allow ourselves to be distracted from our ministry?' Long ago, the Dean of Westminster Cathedral told me and my wife at lunch, 'the tragedy of the time I have left is watching the devil convince the church to fight over human sexuality and keep us from doing the real ministry.'"

At the end of our conversation, Donald attempted to sum up his feelings. "The biggest law is what Jesus said in response to the question of how to inherit eternal life: 'Love God and love your neighbor as yourself.' How can I stand before God and admit I hate my neighbor? How can anyone?"

HOME CHURCH REACTION

When I returned home to Isanti, Minnesota, I had breakfast with my pastor, Howard Skulstad. Howie, as many of us call him, was dispirited about the response at Long Lake Lutheran to the ELCA Task Force on Sexuality report. A group of ten or so had been meeting and wanted to force the church to vote on harsher responses. I termed this the Episcopal response and told Howie about Donald's bishop's experience. Howie feared that this group planned to disrupt the congregational annual meeting which was scheduled for the next Sunday. "They may call for a with-us-or-against-us vote," he said.

It bothered me to see Howie upset, so I called Associate Pastor Andrew Prin, who told me the story of the group and how he facilitated a meeting in January.

"Sixteen to twenty-four people attended, and some did not appear to be satisfied with the recommendations because they didn't call out the sin."

The previous Wednesday the group gathered to talk, and he attended, telling them that he would help them write anything they wanted to present to the forthcoming Minneapolis Area Synod Assembly to be sure it had the proper form. Pastor Andrew said they were meeting the following day, and he saw it as an invitation-only meeting. He felt I should not go.

I decided I had to talk with some of the congregation to find out their logic and thinking. I called Colleen Johnson to see if she had any knowledge of the meetings. She said that she had been invited to attend a meeting on Wednesday evening at Long Lake. She named the man who had invited her and told me of his shock at learning that her son lived with his partner in a then fourteen-year relationship. Colleen invited me to accompany her.

On Wednesday, February 2, 2005, I attended the meeting and sat next to Colleen. The meeting was facilitated by a woman who has asked that I not use her name. She said that Pastor Andrew had given them some instructions on how to submit resolutions to the Synod Assembly.

A member of the church council agreed that most people don't want ordained GLBT or blessings, but he didn't want to create a task force to look at alternative denominations. That set the agenda tone for me.

Another man on the church council presented a motion to have a committee determine what choices are available instead of the ELCA. A woman had another draft that I thought seemed to have more anger in it.

The facilitator said neutrality between good and evil is not possible. I interpreted this as seeing only one side and not allowing others to have a different opinion on Scripture. Being different is evil.

One woman said, "Don't you want the church to represent what the Bible says?"

Others voiced opinions on the issue, but since Colleen didn't say anything and I didn't either, no one spoke for those persons directly affected by the ELCA report. No one at my church had asked to have a same-gender relationship blessed at the church, and this congregation was certainly not going to call someone in such a relationship to be its pastor.

At the end, a vote was taken with the expressed goal of being united on forming a group, independent of the church council, to look at the alternatives. When I voted no, I was asked why. I said I thought the ELCA did many very good things, particularly in mission work and disaster relief, and I wanted to be part of that. And I wondered if I, too, was being silent about the sexuality issues out of fear for my standing in the church.

WHO SAYS IT IS A SIN?

I was curious about the woman who seemed to be the spokesperson for those at Long Lake Lutheran who were upset with the ELCA policies on human sexuality. She asked me not to use her name but did meet me at a local café.

In past dealings, I found her to be compassionate, as she has, several times, shown concern when my wife or I had health issues. I told her about my other books, and how the hate I found at the Long Lake Lutheran sessions disturbed me so much that I wanted to find the reason for it, and how that led to the writing of this book. I asked her why she is so concerned with the ELCA human sexuality study.

After ordering breakfast, she started by saying, "I'm a piece of this church and the policies of the church are a reflection on me. We are to follow Jesus Christ and practice forgiveness, love. GLBT sexual behavior is not loving. Our God cries when he hears or sees it. If my church is part of a larger church, people look at me as though maybe I'm okay with it. I'm not. It is important to me for our pastors and leaders to make a stand for what is right. It is sad that homosexuals are unwelcome and not cared for by the church, and other groups feel the same."

She made a fist, then smiled. "Others feel the same way. Sin is staring us in the face. If they have been in the church from childhood, they know what is taught. You can't make right what is wrong. A person who knows Christ must set an example in our church."

She has been a member of LLLC since 1971, and it is the only church she has attended since moving "up here." She served two three-year terms on church council, leading the youth committee the whole time. She was on council when the last pastor resigned, when Pastor Howard was hired, and when the new building was built.

I mentioned that one of our council members shared with the church council that her daughter is a lesbian in a relationship. I said I was pleased that the daughter was allowed to sing on Christmas Eve in church.

"Why wouldn't she?" she asked.

I replied that the present church council president wouldn't have done anything, but others might have wanted to. She shook her head. "Whatever our sin is, well that's between us and God."

"Then you don't condemn the daughter?"

"Not at all. I taught her in Sunday school. We're all in the ELCA and it is a corporate body, and belief covers all of us. It does bother me that a lesbian pastor is working in [another neighboring] church. I'm not happy that they dropped the sanctions against her church. We build on the Ten Commandments and can learn so much from the Old Testament and history. A lesbian in the pulpit? Where is the credibility? It's like telling a child that curfew is ten p.m. and insisting on it and when the second child comes along we give in and it is okay to stay out later, deviating from the foundation of the family. What's left? We are holding on by a thread."

"We need to be bold. This is what I believe God wants us to do, in my mind, heart, this is part of the ELCA. I could leave it and have chosen not to so far. I was brought up in this denomination by my mom, to believe in a nurturing, reinforcing God. It's about my church." She made a little fist again. "It is my church! God has a plan for me. I just haven't figured out what God wants. We're human beings and have to deal with our shortcomings."

I wondered how she was handling her children at home. I didn't even know how many children she had or what their ages were. I didn't know much about her, other than she had been divorced and remarried and was quite active in our church.

She went on. "Long Lake Lutheran Church is a Christian congregation, a gift of God. The ELCA leaders are not using discretion on how to use the gifts of money. Homosexual acts are a sin. That is the crux of it. We can come to church and learn, but don't pat someone on the back who is sinning. My niece had a terrible time lying, but we confronted her and she doesn't do that anymore. My nephew did drugs at age twenty-five and is recovered. We need to tell them that

God has so much more for them. Put it right up front so they can see the glory."

She then talked about the ELCA and the Federal Marriage Amendment. She believes in the sanctity of marriage between one man and one woman. She wrote the council to have the church and its members contact our elected officials to lobby in favor of it, and the council said, "No, that's political."

"Okay," she said, "I could still do that myself. What irritated and angered me was that within a month the ELCA was lobbying on MY behalf to tell MY congressman that the ELCA opposes the amendment. The corporate church is directly opposite to my congregation, and it wasn't right."

"The Minneapolis Synod took that action," I said, "and they represent over one hundred seventy congregations. Long Lake Lutheran is just one of them. The synod assembly voted for that action. More churches were for it than against it."

She shook her head to say no, as though what I said wasn't true. "The church is afraid," she said, "or the leaders have so much on their minds, they won't take on one more moral issue. We have real, live bodies hurting. The death of a child. Loss of a job. Cancer. Homosexuality. And the sexuality study has been a cop-out. It has been brewing for a long time. Society is forcing this on us. It's so strong, and what are lay people going to do? It is an easier road to let the hot potato go. It is important for lay people to pray for leaders to have wisdom and courage. Talk about it. Do something."

"What would it take to change your mind?" I asked.

"Pastor Andrew and the ELCA study made me stronger in my view, not less. I read a book some years ago by a bishop who had a gay child, and as I read it I thought, maybe I'm not being fair. I may be too judgmental. I need to be open. Four or five years ago I saw how others perceive it. I was in Little Falls for a baptism. In the Northeast Minnesota Synod. I noticed that the synod had an all-day seminar. I talked to my sister's pastor and in five minutes I heard from him what I needed to hear from my own pastor and still haven't. You know, in time we'll be gone. Dead. If we don't say what is wrong, who will? Especially if they haven't heard it? I spent all day at the seminar and learned a lot."

I asked her about the hate I heard and mentioned several of the other women by name who don't come to our church any more. I remembered the passion and how it must have pierced Colleen.

"She was being true to how she reads the Bible."

"Why are they hateful?" I asked.

"It is fear for fellow Christians and the church and where we are going. Is there no condemnation and hell? Pastor Howie is a very compassionate person, but he can let it go too. He gives too much latitude to where we are going with what we do."

I could see she clearly wanted him to condemn homosexual acts.

"The ELCA has set up tension on MY church and there is a threat of leaving the denomination. The whole idea of the denomination as a corporate body is that I want it to reflect what I believe and have been taught from childhood."

So, it boils down to "It's a sin" for her. Again. But does it? She's divorced and remarried, and the Bible sees that as sin, too. Is there something deeper? She mentioned fear as being the motivation behind the hate-sounding talk. What is she afraid of? Being linked to a denomination that is linked to sex? Is it a need for certainty in an uncertain world? Is she making a stand on an issue based on what she sees as a disintegrating society?

She opened her purse and put some money on the table. "That includes the tip for my breakfast. I've got to get to work." She smiled and hurried out the door, heading for her office.

I wondered again, why is one sin special? This intense, sincere woman can say she doesn't treat it differently, and often says, "We all sin." But she wouldn't keep a male and a female from living together for those sins because they would be doing sex acts that are not (necessarily) prohibited. I thought of a former member of Long Lake Lutheran who left in protest over the failure to do more to condemn homosexuality. One of his sons had been living with a woman for over a year, had a child, and only then married in the church. We all may sin, but some sins are forgivable.

Maybe this is what is bothering my judgmental friend and others like her. If we let our adult children live with someone without marriage, is that the step before letting them live with someone of the same gender? Is their resistance based on the fear that our values are being eroded?

Chapter 8

Preparation for Orlando

Although the Churchwide Assembly would not take place until August 2005, in early February I attended a briefing session for the clergy and lay persons who had been elected to be voting members from the Minneapolis Area Synod. The group included an equal number of men and women, and of pastors and lay persons. Rev. Dennis Tollefson, senior pastor of Cambridge Lutheran Church, and I were the two elected from the Northern Conference. Cambridge is the next town north of Isanti, which is the town nearest to my home. We were meeting in the same conference room in the Minnesota Church Center in Minneapolis where the synod council meets.

After Bishop Craig Johnson welcomed us, bishop's associate Glenndy Ose led the session. A large woman with an engaging, sometimes impish smile, and a great sense of humor, Glenndy requested that we develop an ability to live together in harmony.

"Remember, it is never safe to assume that others aren't trying just as hard as we are, even if we disagree about the issues before the Assembly." Then she read a list she created from reading *Background Essay of Biblical Texts* (Hultgren and Taylor, 2003). She said there are six ways to read the ethical guidance in Scripture:

1. *Sacred Cow:* one cannot touch the text at all. It is revealed morality.
2. *Traditional:* human nature is essentially constant from time to time over centuries, and culture does not shape interpretation.
3. *Neo-traditional:* some Scripture is to be read within the cultural context, such as where Paul says women are to be silent in church is read with Paul's all one in Christ, slave & free, etc.
4. *Source of Principles:* read Scripture to understand the moral and ethical overriding principles through the lens of Jesus, like the

Hate Is The Sin

commandment he gave us to love God and our neighbor as ourselves.

5. *Source of identity and a dialogue resource:* from where our faith came, like the more traditional sources of faith, but doesn't limit our inclusivity in a pluralistic society.
6. *White Elephant:* uncomfortable with it and wish it would go away, rather than exerting influence on our moral choices.

We divided into groups of five to discuss where we each were on the list. I decided I fit in categories three and four. I read Scripture in its cultural context, first asking "What did God say at the time of the writing?" I also look at it through the lens of Jesus, asking "What does God say in our particular circumstances today?" I like to call this liberation theology biblical analysis.

Several in my group identified as traditional, and didn't want to re-interpret texts each time they were read. One pastor said that the Scriptures were clear and unambiguous, but didn't like the term 'sacred cow.' "The Bible is the inspired, inerrant word of God." That settled it for him.

We also had a discussion on whether or not there is scientific evidence of gay orientation being fixed and not a choice. The study guide gives a variety of positions but concludes, "Even researchers who take a conservative view of the data and support this church's traditional position on homosexual conduct agree that there is a percentage of people for whom homosexual orientation is not a choice." One pastor in my group said that homosexuality is a sin and argued that, "One can do away with promiscuity and pornography using the same logic as is being used on homosexuality. I have lust for beautiful women I see, but I do nothing about it, other than to put it out of my mind."

I mentioned that I had read a statement that calls out an action to be a sin by a subgroup of humans, and the caller is not a member of the subgroup, is neither biblically sound nor theologically valid. How can we say that some homosexual acts such as oral sex are a sin when those same acts are not a sin for heterosexuals? I asked if seeing two men or two women kiss made them uncomfortable? I shared that twenty years ago when I saw two men dancing together, like I dance with my wife, I was uncomfortable. I added that it was at a party given at the Witherspoon Society, a social justice organization of the Presbyterian Church (USA).

This led a woman to observe that the strongest argument some people have against the report recommendations is that they ask, "What is next? Is bestiality going to be okay?"

The rest of the orientation meeting dealt with logistics. I think most of us felt good having calm discussions where we respected the views of others with whom we did not agree.

After the meeting I went back to one of the books I've read on this subject. A scholarly work, *Christianity, Social Tolerance, and Homosexuality, Gay People in Western Europe from the Beginning of the Christian era to the Fourteenth Century,* by John Boswell (1980) has some helpful observations. Boswell writes:

> If religious strictures are used to justify oppression by people who regularly disregard precepts of equal gravity from the same moral code, or if prohibitions which restrain a disliked minority are upheld in their most literal sense as absolutes inviolable while comparable precepts affecting the majority are relaxed or reinterpreted, one must suspect something other than religious belief as the motivating cause of the oppression. (p. 7)

Boswell discussed hypocrisy as a much more condemned action, as is greed. "And yet no medieval states burned the greedy at the stake."

After meeting and talking with so many people while researching this book, it would be impossible for me to have not formed an opinion regarding human sexuality. I am unable to ignore what Anglican Archbishop and Nobel Peace Laureate Desmond Tutu said, "Not taking sides is taking sides." I don't think it is likely that society will return to a time when all sin is condemned, if that time ever existed. We are too diverse to allow moral police to run our lives, lest we go the way of the Taliban in Afghanistan. It is no longer possible in American culture for divorce, cohabitation between heterosexual adults, and so on, to be a barrier to full inclusion into society. For that reason I think society in general, and the ELCA specifically, will, in time, also fully accept persons in committed, long-term, same-sex unions for all aspects of life in the ELCA, including ordination of otherwise qualified candidates.

AN OPEN MICROPHONE

On April 16, 2005, the Minneapolis Area Synod held its annual assembly, meeting at the Shepherd of the Lake Lutheran Church in suburban Prior Lake, Minnesota. The church, really a campus, has a large sanctuary where the voting members sat. I attended because of my position on the Synod Council. I sat with three lay people from my church and the associate pastor, Andrew Prin. Senior pastor Howard Skulstad joined us late in the session.

At one point, the moderator, Bishop Craig Johnson, declared the Assembly to be a committee of the whole, and set a one-hour time for an open microphone session. We were asked to express our thoughts on the recommendations of the Human Sexuality Task Force report. People were polite, took their turns, kept to the time limit, and some showed great passion. These are some of the remarks I recorded in my notebook.

> "My cousin was gay, tried suicide, went to the Bible, found no affirmation of his lifestyle, but saw signs to the right path."
>
> "Luther taught us to study, and now that leads to a new time for the church. We must work together with our differences."
>
> "My concern is about how sexuality is handled. Genesis is ignored. Children are left out of the debate. Gays shouldn't marry because male and female parents are best for children. Same-sex acts are wrong."
>
> "We are going the wrong way, and need more respect for change, rather than the passive recommendations. False unity is divisive."
>
> "Eighteen years ago we accepted divorce and no one sin is worse than any other."
>
> "We are seeing the living word versus the written word. Are we limiting the work of reconciliation?"
>
> "Go and sin no more. Don't keep on sinning. We are struggling with what culture says versus what God says. It is like saying, 'I do pornography and God made me that way.'"
>
> "Are all of us created as one, except . . .?"
>
> "Congregations should have the right to choose."
>
> "Read Romans 1-3. Unless gays and lesbians accept responsibility for the sin they won't get well."

"We need law and gospel, not one or the other."
"The Bible isn't our guide, Christ is."
"Slavery one-hundred sixty years ago was right, based on the Bible."
"We ordained women thirty-five years ago."
"Homosexuality is a sin and God died for our sins."
"Thirty-five years ago the church changed, supported ordination of women, then came acceptance of divorced clergy. Homosexual sex is wrong. It's different."

Then the debate began for Resolution Number Three, which authorized covenanting committed same-gender relationships. People spoke for and against this resolution.

"This encourages churches to violate law, and leads to confusion and compromise."
"I am heterosexual and can't have children, and my marriage is as good as any. Same should be for homosexuals."
"I've done hospice for twenty-seven years, and had four hundred AIDS deaths. The gay and lesbian lifestyle is rotten."
In favor: "Some acts are condemned, both ways."
"It is secular and two percent of gays remain monogamous, and the church is trying to force an agenda."
"Compare heterosexual weddings with the book of Ruth."

This resolution passed by a vote of 302 in favor, 257 opposed, and 23 abstentions.

We then debated Resolution Number Four, which affirmed the Task Force recommendations. Again, voting members spoke for and against this resolution.

"I come from a RIC (Reconciling In Christ) congregation with many GLBT in the congregation. Some will leave if the barrier is not removed."
"These recommendations go beyond what is right and divide the church and damage ecumenism."
"In Christ for faith, we all are sanctified. Who does God love and who does God not love?"
"There is no need for change."

"Some places have passed it."

"Grace without courage and turning decisions over to a local option is cheap grace."

This resolution also passed, this time by 307 in favor, 257 against, and 16 abstentions.

Resolution Number Five specifically authorized ordination of gays and lesbians in committed relationships. This debate included the following comments.

"This is scriptural and within Jesus' teaching. Let's stay in honest dialogue together."

"This acts as though it is a done deal, and is a preemptive approach. We are divided and this will make it worse. It is not consensus building."

"I have deep roots in ELCA, and I am worried that we only let the Holy Spirit enforce the past. But to deny this implies that the Holy Spirit can't work now."

"The last two votes show how we are divided. We're in fellowship with the United Church of Christ and the Episcopal Church, and will be forced to pull out of fellowship with a long list of denominations."

"We have two gay couples in our congregation who do good things, and Christ is visible in them. They help all of us."

The last speaker read from Augsburg Catechism and read from scripture.

The vote defeated the resolution with 269 in favor, 300 against, and 17 abstaining. The next debate was on Resolution Number Six, which called for affirmation of the present.

"Visions and Expectations" rules of pastoral conduct was cited by several speakers.

"Statistics in the ELCA report affirm these guidelines and we want a reasoned biblical and theological basis for any change, and there isn't any."

"This was approved by a vote of 25 to 17 at the Northwestern Conference assembly and it was brought with improper procedure. It shouldn't even be considered."

> "This is biblical. We don't ignore the past. We don't approve of homosexual acts but accept homosexuals in our church."
> "We speak as a church here, and where two or more are gathered, God is with us."
> "We need a study of these resolutions and need much more study."

The next speaker was Jay Wiesner. "When I heard my call to the ministry and when I learned I was gay, both were obvious to others who knew me. To ignore one is to do violence to my soul."

This resolution failed by a vote of 228 for, 342 against, with no abstentions.

The assembly went on to other agenda items, having debated and decided all it would about human sexuality. August was the Churchwide Assembly.

EFFECT OF THE ELCA COUNCIL

There was something we didn't discuss at the assembly that I thought important. Three days before the assembly, on April 11, the ELCA Church Council announced its own recommendations. We discussed them briefly at the Synod Council meeting on April 14. Bishop's Associate Rev. Jerry Wahl gave a short summary. Basically, the first recommendation remained the same, which is that the ELCA members concentrate on finding ways to live together faithfully in the midst of these disagreements. The second recommendation, on blessing same-sex relationships, affirmed the same 1993 statement of the Conference of Bishops and added that the church should "welcome gay and lesbian persons into its life . . . and trust pastors and congregations to discern ways to provide faithful pastoral care to same-sex couples."

The third recommendation changed things. While affirming the current "Visions and Expectations" for most pastors, it created a process for an exception for gay and lesbian candidates and rostered leaders in "life-long, committed, and faithful same-sex relationships who otherwise are determined to be in compliance with 'Visions and Expectations.'"

Near the end of the assembly I spoke briefly with Bishop Craig Johnson, asking why we didn't tell the voting members about the ELCA Church Council's change in the Sexuality Task Force recommendations. He said he considered bringing it up but decided not to because the voting members had prepared to debate and vote on the Task Force recommendations, and it was important that they express their opinions on what they had considered. It seemed like a good decision. I know the people from Long Lake Lutheran had done their homework and voted their conscience on each resolution. I later learned that no one objected to the decision. Bishop Johnson was right; people wanted to vote on what they had studied.

Chapter 9

A Solid Rock Lutheran

There are groups who don't agree with the ELCA Church Council. One such group, Solid Rock Lutherans, is an organization formed with the mission: "To call the Evangelical Lutheran Church in America to remain faithful to the Word of God according to the Lutheran Confessions." Solid Rock's Web site stated: "We are dedicated to upholding the current biblical and confessional standards on sexual conduct and ordination. We believe that the Word of God affirms the union of woman and man in the bonds of marriage and that only those who are guided by this Word be considered for ordination."

In April 2005, Solid Rock representatives had met with the ELCA Church Council before the Council revised the Task Force recommendations. The Web site noted the Council vote of 32 to 2 that spelled out the exceptional ordination procedure that would, under specified conditions, allow gays or lesbians to be ordained and installed. Solid Rock said, "The Church Council has, by virtue of this action, redefined Christian identity, rejected traditional marriage, created a double standard, and provided for unlimited exceptions across the ELCA. It has proven that it is out of touch with the Church."

Solid Rock had been formed to oppose this kind of change in the ELCA, so it was no surprise that it had a strong reaction to the ELCA action. I wanted to find out how strong, so I made an appointment to meet with Rev. Dr. Roy A. Harrisville III to talk about his organization and its opposition to ordaining clergy in committed same-sex unions. He has been a pastor, teacher, Greek instructor at a seminary, and has his MDiv from Luther in St. Paul, and his PhD from Union Seminary in Richmond, Virginia. He served half-time as the executive director of Solid Rock Lutherans. My initial impression was that he was friendly, knowledgeable, and sincere.

Hate Is The Sin

I told Roy that as a voting member for the upcoming Churchwide Assembly, I had read his mailings, looked at his Web site, and wanted to hear more. He explained that it was important for the ELCA to have only "one pool from which to draw pastors. We want to influence the church to maintain its standards. We are supported in our position by Scripture and by public health issues."

I brought up my regular topic. "What do you have to say about the hate being expressed?"

"There is hate on both sides. Hate always comes from the devil. I don't care to get close to the hate. I try to be gracious and positive yet firm. I took Jen Nagel to lunch and we had a fine time."

"I know her," I said. Jen Nagel is in a committed same-gender relationship, has graduated from seminary, and serves in a Minneapolis church. I knew her from the Minneapolis Area Synod Council where she represents the Partnership Table. I said, "Jen says she has no choice in how she feels about her partner."

Roy seemed to be upset that I didn't start the discussion from where he wanted to start it. "It is important," he said sharply, "to frame the starting point. We don't talk about orientation. The issue is behavior. Sexual practices. To allow the ordination of gays and lesbians under any circumstance, the church has to first say the Bible is wrong, and second, that the way you are born is the way you should be." Roy doesn't accept that homosexuals are born that way. That rejects the transformation we have through Christ. "Look at behavior, never at orientation."

I wryly thought that I hadn't heard such a stern tone since grade school. He told me, not asked me, to start with his premise of "homosexual acts" and not orientation. It helped me to understand his argument, to listen to his premise and the logic, but it was no way to have a dialogue. Of course, I was there to learn what he thought, not to debate. I mentioned that I felt my attraction for my wife didn't require a rejection of Christ.

"It isn't the same," he replied. "Sodomy is always wrong."

"I have never thought about sodomy with my wife."

"I should hope not," he said, staring at me.

"There is no sodomy with lesbians, is there?" I was curious.

"What women do is not life-threatening. Besides, most lesbians become so from sexual abuse as a young girl. They are just shy from men."

When I left Solid Rock's office and transcribed my notes, I wondered about Roy. What motivates someone who is ordained and has a PhD to devote half his working time opposing gay and lesbian committed relationships based on Scripture and concerning an act that only the male half of the GLBT can even do? I have no doubt that he is sincere. The role of Scripture is at the very center of his debate. I continued to wonder why so many people not directly affected by the issue are so obsessed with the outcome.

MY PASTOR

After talking with Dr. Harrisville, I met with Pastor Andrew Prin, associate pastor of Long Lake Lutheran Church. I asked him how the congregation's study started.

"Back in March 2003, the Long Lake Lutheran Church Council got a letter complaining that the church wasn't dealing with the human sexuality study and there was no forum for a discussion. Pastor Howard and I both said, 'If the people want a study, here are the parameters. We aren't going to have a free-for-all.' We created an over-reaching scheme first. After that we decided to be proactive. We as a church should never be afraid to talk about any topic."

When I expressed appreciation for his leadership under difficult circumstances and mentioned the hate I felt, Pastor Andrew added, "I wanted to improve my moderating skills without getting in the trench. I stressed that everyone is attempting to faithfully determine what the issues are and how they should be resolved."

Pastor Andrew referred to Luther's comments on the eighth commandment, saying, "We must defend our neighbor and explain their position in the best and kindest possible way. Stay united in Christ even though we disagree. Pastor Howard and I decided to start each session with worship, and end on our knees at communion. You could feel the tension being relaxed last time."

I remembered being on my knees for communion, and I recalled that some of those most outspoken against gays and lesbians didn't stay for the sacrament.

PASTOR DAVID GLESNE'S BOOK

The evening after I met with Roy, I attended another session of the Minneapolis Area Synod voting member orientation. I briefly spoke to Jen Nagel and told her Roy enjoyed taking her to lunch. I got a different reaction from her. "He doesn't understand," she said.

I also met and sat with Pastor David Glesne. I had purchased David's book after the Synod Assembly, and I had finished reading it. In my reading I noted that a "reasoned" biblical and theological basis requires adoption of a premise, and that once that premise is adopted, the logic is fairly straightforward. For example, David has used the creation texts of taking a rib from Adam to form Eve to justify heterosexual nature. He is using Genesis 1-2 creation narrative as a literal truth, not as a myth. When the myth becomes fact, the conclusions follow.

Glesne has put a lot of time into his narrative, marshalling his thoughts to persuade. His faith statements of how Christ is in our lives are intended to be inclusive. On page 71, he tells of a Japanese woman befriended by co-workers who gave her a Bible in Japanese, and they witnessed to her. Then he wrote, "In that long process the [Japanese] woman was able gradually to put herself in the shoes of those to whom the Bible was written, to understand the love of God in Christ for her, and happily has come to trust Christ as Savior. It can be a difficult road, but the gap can be bridged."

But, I thought, she is still Japanese. Would not a lesbian still be the same if she converted to Christianity?

I read the Bible by first looking at the text to see what God was saying to those at the time of the passages. Then I look at the context of the present time and see what that same text says today. Glesne is in agreement with me on the first part, but not the second. According to him, we must then look at the text by removing our "glasses," which consist of our understanding of culture. That is the opposite of what I do, discarding the context rather than seeing how the context affects what is to be interpreted. Page 74 talks about other lenses—such as process theology, existentialism, liberation theology and so on—being bad lenses that distort the meaning. On page 75, Glesne writes, "Reading the Bible through these glasses does not allow the Bible to speak for itself but in fact construes the Bible to say something that it does not say."

Also on page 75 he talks about a woman in a terribly abusive relationship with her husband. She finally leaves him after reading, "Wives, be subject to your husband as you are to the Lord." He counsels her to ignore the text. He does not suggest that she should stay in the abuse, but that is implied. He ignores her context, where she is seeking God's guidance to relieve suffering (be liberated) and still follow Christ. He writes, "In this case the abusive personal experience has become the 'alternative philosophy,' the lens that does not allow Paul to speak for himself."

On pages 75-76 David writes of a gay man who follows his feelings and enters a long-term, same-gender relationship filled with love. David uses the gay man's reading of Leviticus to illustrate how a lens says Leviticus isn't talking to him, but to heterosexuals. Again personal experience prevents a literal reading of the text.

The debate going on in the church is about interpreting Scripture. Why do people care about homosexuals in decent relationships? Why is this sin any different than racism, divorce, exploitation of the poor, the death penalty, abortion, greed, gluttony, ignoring disease and tragedy? Why should we not read the Bible from our own personal experiences?

Over and over I have asked myself, "Where is the fear coming from?" One thought is that people are scared that if the snake didn't actually talk, then Noah's ark was a mythic story, and Jesus didn't walk on water or rise from the dead. Is that a necessary conclusion? I remember my Mennonite friends who were scared that if any of the Bible wasn't true then none of it might be. Is that where the fear is coming from?

Pastor David Glesne's book is as much about interpretation as it is about the human sexuality issues. He says,

> There would be two warnings here. First, the Holy Spirit does not communicate to us any doctrine not already contained in Scripture. The Holy Spirit makes us wise up to what is written— not beyond. The Psalmist asked that God would open his eyes to understand what is *already there*. When the Church sets the Word against the Spirit, at that point it borders on becoming cultic. The Word is nullified from judging claims to any new revelation. There is no new revelation beyond Scripture. (p. 76)

David writes,

> Second, inspiration is infallible, but illumination is not. Inspiration is the Holy Spirit, without in any way abrogating the humanness and personalities of the authors, moving the human writers along in their understanding. Illumination is not infallible. God has chosen to give us a God-breathed, wholly accurate book but not inerrant understanding. Even though we pray for God to give us understanding, it does not mean that our understanding is infallible. We have no such guarantee. (p. 77)

This is a clear statement of the views of many in the ELCA. David is a pleasant man, friendly and accepting of individuals. He represents the best of those who oppose the struggle of gays and lesbians on unions and ordination. But this is not objective.

I thought about David when I read a book review in the *Washington Post National Weekly Edition* of June 12, 2005, by Mark Oppenheimer. The piece starts out, "Many authors who write about the Bible are so tendentious that their books are worthless; other writers are thoughtful and well meaning but nonetheless argue as much from faith as from evidence." The reviewer then reviews three books related to ancient texts that did not deal with sexuality.

When I look at David's book, he argues that God intended male and female to be the only relationship because God took Eve from Adam's body, forming his rib into woman. The premise is that the story is true and literal. But if humans evolved over the millennia, then Genesis is a myth (perhaps "theological metaphor" would be a more acceptable phrase) that relates an understanding of creation from a theological perspective, not from science. The premise that God historically took Eve from Adam's body to make the first couple is false. David writes that God saw that Adam was lonely and that God, for the first time, says that something was not good. From that he reasons that since God gave Adam a woman, that was the only partner (or other person to alleviate loneliness) that God intended men to have. That reasoning is valid if one understands that the context is of a heterosexual male doing the reasoning and taking his orientation as normative.

My view of the creation story in Genesis relates to when it was written (obviously long after Adam and Eve's days), people believed everything came from God, including male and female, and that the text formed part of that current worldview. That same worldview in Genesis believes that the earth is flat and the sky is a dome. My worldview of today includes evolution, not creationism. Leaving aside whether or not there is an intelligent design behind evolution, God is the creator (as a matter of faith) of everything we know, and how God did that (as a matter of science) involves evolution.

As people like me read Genesis now, we see that we have been created in God's image. I believe that a gay man can also read Genesis and see that he, too, has been created in God's image. To say as David does, that after the fall imperfections and mistakes came into the world to explain why some people have a sexual orientation that is a mistake, is to bring into the present reading what is not there. To say as I would, that in the present time there are people whose sexual orientation is different from mine is no different than to say there are people with musical abilities that are different from mine, and that there are shorter and taller people, smarter and not as smart, kinder and more nasty people.

There is a bias in the writing. David describes John Spong as a "liberal" Episcopal bishop and John Howe as a "conservative-leaning" Episcopal bishop. Why make the distinction? David says he is not homophobic; he doesn't have a fear of homosexuals. Fear, not hate, is his word; it is a more accurate use of phobic but ignores the hate so many have. Don't gays and lesbians read the Bible? While it does condemn adultery and fornication, and sodomy as Harrisville says, it does not condemn loving, committed, long-term marriages. Or so I would argue.

There is another aspect to David's book. In a long article in the May 23, 2005, *New Yorker* magazine by staff writer Michael Specter, Specter writes that methamphetamine is now the drug of choice in the gay scene. The conduct of the men described in the article justifies the refusal of the church to ordain gays who are not celibate. Just as the church will defrock someone for molesting a child or having an extra-marital affair or even from improper use of pornography, participation in the gay culture of multiple partners is also a reason for keeping someone from a position of church leadership.

This helps me understand David's book, because he has rejected the same conduct that Specter describes. David also writes about graphic sex acts, some of which are as unacceptable to heterosexuals as they are to homosexuals and some or all may be practiced by both orientations in deviate form. He doesn't address acts that are tender, kind, and loving between persons who are partners. I haven't found any theological or biblical basis in his book for rejection of these persons. For that reason, I believe the debate shifts from general acceptance of gays to specific acceptance of individuals.

In another long essay titled "What's Their Real Problem With Gay Marriage," by Russell Shorto, the author begins with Genesis 2:18-25 where God makes a partner for Adam. The essay ends with two women. One is a lesbian and the other is a committed Christian working against homosexuality. The essay concludes with each woman describing how the Christian asked why the lesbian was "doing this" to her children and grandchildren. Shorto writes, "I realized I was hearing about the same encounter from both sides. What was expressed as love was received as something close to hate. That's a hard gap to bridge," (p. 67). Shorto is so right.

Chapter 10

Welcome to Orlando

I flew to Orlando, Florida, on August 8, 2005, to take part in the ELCA Churchwide Assembly. There were other voting members on the plane and we engaged in "getting to know you" conversations. Bad weather delayed the flight from Minneapolis, and poor ground transportation delayed the transfer in Orlando from the airport to the hotel and convention center complex.

After checking into our rooms, we took our foot-thick workbooks through the maze that led to the convention center and found our place. The Minneapolis Area Synod, the largest in the ELCA, took up more than two rows of seating. We each had an electronic voting device. When activated, we could vote by simply pushing a button for yes or no, then confirm the vote.

That evening we began the first working session. Before any substantive work took place, we had to resolve procedural matters. Do we need two-thirds or a simple majority to amend or pass resolutions and amendments to resolutions? The debates raged on. I quickly saw that there were two groups of advocates, each well-prepared to put forth arguments for their position. On one side, Good Soil argued for change. On the other, Solid Rock argued against change.

Those advocating for change wanted simple majority decisions for church treatment of homosexual couples. They had formed Good Soil, describing it as a coordinated effort of six organizations "to end the ELCA's policy of discrimination." One of the partners was the Extraordinary Candidacy Project, which had ordained and installed Jay Wiesner at Bethany Lutheran Church. Other partners were Lutheran Lesbian & Gay Ministries, Lutherans Concerned/North America, Lutheran Network for Inclusive Vision, Wingspan Ministry of Reformation Lutheran Church in St. Paul, Minnesota, and Soulforce, an interfaith movement.

Solid Rock's view was that no basis for change had been made and that biblical and theological reasons existed for keeping the traditional rules and policies on human sexuality as applied to unions and ordination.

During the debate, a former bishop addressed the assembly. "If it is God's will it will happen. We dealt with divorce, and never had a vote on divorce. A pastor came to me to tell me he is divorcing his wife. I said, 'Give me your resignation. Go back to your church. If the congregation says stay, at least eighty-five percent, okay. If not, I'll ask the council to accept the resignation.'"

Both sides had well-articulated positions and some of the votes were very close. When we were scheduled to adjourn, we voted to extend the session, first to 7:30 p.m., then to 8:30 p.m. We finally adjourned at 12:30 a.m. We were all quite tired, and it was only the first day.

At breakfast the next morning, I sat with two bishops and a pastor. One bishop talked about the recent Conference of Bishops meeting. I asked him why the bishops couldn't agree on the human sexuality issues.

He said, "Really, the bishops are fun, and enjoy each other. There is great disagreement but wonderful collegiality."

I asked for that to be communicated. I told him, "I understood that they couldn't even agree on the first recommendation that asks us to stay together in this struggle. They could issue no statement." I told him the church needs to know that there is unity in something.

The pastor at breakfast, from the Southeastern Minnesota Synod, said, "We're seated on the far right. Seems Minneapolis should be on the far left." He wasn't joking.

During his opening remarks that morning, Presiding Bishop Mark Hanson said that there is "too much fear of a radical proclamation of the Gospel." I understood that Bishop Hanson had a very difficult task, to moderate debates that had caused great stress and conflict in the denomination. It quickly became clear that he saw his work as trying to be fair, open, and unbiased. He worked very hard to guide the assembly without influencing it. True, I wanted him to take a position, but he served the church better with his impartiality.

WAGING THE DEBATE

That morning I asked the voting member sitting next to me, "If we can't solve pronoun problems, how can we deal with the sexuality of committed couples?"

During the discussion on the new hymnbook some people objected to inclusive language and loss of words like "king" and "Lord" and "His" and "He." I felt the strident minority, no more than 25 percent with probably a core of 10 percent, did not trust the ELCA. This issue arose because we approved the hymnal before its completion, negating the need to vote on it when it finally comes out. The majority of voting members seemed to trust the ELCA, but some did not.

That evening the Task Force for ELCA Studies on Sexuality held hearings where questions could be asked and persons could express their opinions and concerns. Here are some of the comments I recorded in my notebook.

> "When Jesus comes again, it won't be at a Churchwide Assembly."
>
> "The second resolution is ambiguous and that is intentional, so that the church will trust the guidance of pastoral care by pastors."
>
> "The second recommendation is nothing new but its strength is in understanding the benefit of paradox."
>
> "I want the congregation to call the pastors, not the bishops."
>
> "I'm a retired physician and I have had success with reparative therapy in over fifty percent of my cases in treating homosexuals."
>
> A task force member said, "We were sensitive, and had respect for one another's consciences and shared the same sense of being faithful to them."
>
> "Orientation is not a problem but sexual activity is the sin."
>
> "I am a gay woman. The church is responsible for its effect on real people. The church kept me out of seminary."
>
> "This is about G & L. What about B & T?"
>
> "If these resolutions pass, our ties with Africa may have to be broken. How does this affect our ties to the Lutheran World Federation?"

> "It is an issue of evangelism. Remember those we lost. Voting
> members should talk evangelism. We need to be open and the
> grace of God is to all people."
>
> "There is a failure to reach a good biblical study by focusing on
> the seven texts. We can't get outside the box. What about
> other texts?"
>
> "I am a gay son of a conservative Missouri Synod minister. I asked
> my father, 'Do you want to understand, Dad?' He said, 'No.'"

Although the Assembly began on a Monday, we did not cover the human sexuality issues until Friday. The debates were intense, sincerely felt and, sometimes, heartbreaking.

An Asian-appearing man said that the Lutheran Church refused to allow his marriage many years ago because of a verse in Leviticus 19. A woman said that she had been reading a romance novel, felt passion and was aroused, and the church saved her from confusion about her orientation. A man said that he was gay and also was a third-generation pastor, and he refuses to be banished.

In regards to the second recommendation, to allow pastors to handle same-gender unions, a bishop stated that there is no support in the Conference of Bishops for blessing same-gender unions.

Another pastor said, "We voted for ordination of women thirty-five years ago, and found compelling reasons to set aside Paul's writings. In 1972, divorce kept pastors out. We had the words of Jesus condemning divorce, and yet we found compelling reasons to change the rules."

A man identified himself as gay, then said he asked for transformation, went to reparative therapy, had demons exorcised, and has had a twenty year struggle that didn't work. "I accept myself and I have a caring pastor who also accepts me for who I am."

Another man identified himself as German. "We hold tensions and express our faith, and talk about sexuality. Good theology is needed, not biblical fundamentalism."

Another pastor asked that all but voting members be excluded, saying that he had threats of intimidation, and some are taking it seriously.

A layperson asked, "When you see the humanity of a person, when you find them to be interesting, do you really think about what they do in the bedroom?"

Then we voted.

The first human sexuality resolution dealt with getting along and staying united as a denomination. It passed nicely, with 851 for and 127 against—87 percent in favor.

The second human sexuality resolution dealt with pastoral care for same-gender unions, or it did, until the voting members passed an amendment changing "faithful pastoral care to same-sex couples" to read "faithful pastoral care to all to whom they minister."

At the time I saw that as good and inclusive language by not making same-sex couples different from anyone else. But others said that because it didn't say 'same-sex couples' it didn't apply to them or that it watered down the import of the matter. In practice, the resolution did not change the fact that ELCA pastors do what they think is right about same-sex couples or heterosexual couples, subject to their congregations and church councils. During the debates on this resolution, half-a-dozen bishops spoke, saying they were at the 1993 Conference of Bishops meeting and it meant this or that to them. They don't agree on that either.

The Solid Rock argument, also held by Pastor David Glesne, is based on the characterization of sexual practices between same-gender persons as being self-gratification. "You can't love Jesus if you love your homosexual partner." They don't have an answer for me when I say I love my female wife in the same way that Pastor Jay Wiesner, for example, loves his partner, Tim, or Pastor Mary Albing loves her partner, Jane. They say that in Genesis 2, God says male and female should cling to each other and in Genesis 1 be fruitful and multiply.

Later I did some reading on that part of Genesis. In *Martin Luther's Basic Theological Writings,* edited by Timothy F. Lull (2005), Luther talks about one exception that may apply to today's issues. He wrote a sermon in 1522, reprinted in Lull's book, on *The Estate of Marriage,* in which he discusses Matthew 19:12, "There are eunuchs who have been so since birth, and there are eunuchs who have been eunuchs by men, and there are eunuchs who have made themselves eunuchs for the sake of the kingdom of heaven" (p. 147). Luther then says, "Apart from these three groups, let no man presume to be without a spouse." Further on, Luther says,

> As to the first category, which Christ calls 'eunuchs who have been so from birth,' these are the ones who men call impotent,

who are by nature not equipped to produce seed and multiply because they are physically sick or weak or have some other bodily deficiency which makes them unfit for the estate of marriage. Such cases occur among both men and women. These we need not take into account, for God has himself exempted them and so formed them that the blessing of being able to multiply has not come to them. The injunction, 'be fruitful and multiply,' does not apply to them; just as when God creates a person crippled or blind, that person is not obligated to walk or see, because he cannot. (p. 148)

Is that different from the gay or lesbian who is also not able to multiply and is that person also exempted and so formed by God? If one starts with orientation, Luther's answer might apply.

The vote was 670 in favor and 323 against the amended resolution. That margin, just over 67 percent in favor, made me wonder if something positive was happening. This and the first resolution needed only a simple majority yet both had passed by a large majority. Because the third resolution needed a two-thirds majority to pass, and because the second resolution had just slightly more than that, it occurred to me that it had a chance.

The last human sexuality resolution dealt with ordination and installation for Word and Sacrament ministry of persons otherwise qualified and in same-gender relationships. It made exceptions for people such as Pastor Jay Wiesner at Bethany and Pastor Mary Albing at LCCR. An ad hoc committee was formed by Presiding Bishop Hanson to put the many amendments in order for consideration by the assembly so that the most radical changes would be considered first.

The first amendment, clearly most radical from the original resolution, called for full recognition of same-gender couples and allowed for their normal and regular ordination and call. That was defeated by 326 yes and 617 no, only receiving 38 percent approval.

After this vote, 100 or so protesters came into the area reserved for voting members. They came from the visitor's section to the front of the stage and stood, silently, arms folded, most wearing rainbow sashes or stoles, in protest. Presiding Bishop Hanson asked them to leave, ordered them to leave, then when it became apparent that they weren't leaving, he announced that as "an experienced parent and grandparent, some things need to be ignored." He said he could continue in spite of them, we agreed, and five minutes later we were back to business. Jay Wiesner would later say that the protests meant "we're here and we're not going away."

Most of us forgot the protestors, but there was one amazing exception. A man came to the mike and asked the bishop to have the protestors removed by force. The bishop declined. What shocked me was that this was an African-American man. I could not help but be amazed at someone who might not have been allowed to be at this assembly if Martin Luther King and the civil rights movement had not used nonviolent protest to break down racial barriers. I found it a symbol of what I think is the true issue: We see what we want for ourselves and refuse to see what is good for others. That is not what Jesus said. "This is my commandment, that you love one another as I have loved you." (John 15:12) The debate remains.

All amendments to this third resolution failed, and the amendment calling for delay on this until the 2009 social statement lost 194 to 808. It was the clearest of any vote on sexuality issues. Resolution 3 eventually was defeated by a vote of 490 to 503, not quite 50 percent in support. I spoke with Good Soil folk later and some of their people voted no because it calls for an exception for gays and lesbians, not full acceptance. They believed there was no chance for a two-thirds majority.

REJECTING OTHER FORMS OF OPPRESSION?

I spoke with a number of people during my time at the Assembly. At one lunch after the first vote on an amendment to Resolution Number Three that would have eliminated the barrier for ordination and installation for candidates in same-gender unions, a woman told me that she had been raised in the Missouri Synod Lutheran Church, which is much more conservative. I asked her why she left that denomination.

"I got a divorce. Then I remarried and I was forbidden to take communion."

"Do you understand that this stridency comes from the way the Missouri Synod leaders read the Bible? Jesus is fairly explicit about divorce. Remarried people are adulterers. Like me," I said, hopefully softening the statement. "The ELCA has a different position and that's what I accept. I'm here as a voting member."

"The ELCA also ordains women," I continued, "Bishop Margaret Payne has led us in worship. We've also heard some good preaching from other women as well as men. You're comfortable with that, too, then?"

"I am. Why?"

"The Missouri Synod reads the Bible to say that women are not to be ordained. Do you have an opinion on the sexuality recommendations?" This was the question I asked most people.

"I can't see it," she said, shaking her head. "I grew up reading the Bible a certain way. I can't throw that away."

"You tossed out divorce." I smiled more, not wanting my words to sting. "And I waited to bring this up until after the vote, because I didn't want to influence you."

"I know. But it is so clear to me. The Bible doesn't allow homosexuality."

"I have talked with a number of people about how the Bible does or doesn't address this issue, and it seems to me that a case can be made, based on one's own context."

"Not for me."

"I hope you take this right. I'm not trying to argue with you or convince you to change your mind about anything. It just seems to me that you left the Missouri Synod because of what you saw as oppression against those who are divorced, and now you should really rethink other forms of oppression."

"I know, but I can't."

"It may be a good idea if you talked to someone who is gay or lesbian about how he or she reads the Bible. It really isn't any different than the way you now interpret Scriptures regarding adultery, which is what you and I are both doing since we're divorced and remarried. If we read the Bible the way you grew up reading it, we're adulterers."

"I don't think it is the same," she replied. "But I will talk to someone about how they read the Bible." We parted as friends.

This, I believe, is the key to the whole debate. If you read the Bible literally and from a heterosexual context, you are on one side. If you allow others to read the Bible from their own context, as, for example, one who is divorced, remarried, and ordained to Word and Sacrament, maybe you can see the context that others have. If you are a gay man like Jay Wiesner, you will have a much different context than a straight man.

After returning to Minnesota, I talked with Pastor Mary Albing. She asked, "Jack, when do you think this will be seen as a justice issue and not about sexuality?"

I had no answer for her. My initial reaction was to wonder if reframing the question into a justice issue and challenging the ELCA and other churches to make that shift in analysis could be the answer. When slavery was debated was there a shift from literal biblical approval of slavery to the issue of justice? When women's ordination and acceptance of divorce occurred, was there a shift from literal biblical interpretations of specific texts to the issue of what is just?

Chapter 11

Vancouver

In August 2005, three days after the ELCA Churchwide Assembly ended, my wife and I flew to Vancouver, Canada, for the World International Bereavement Conference. We were presenting a workshop on how grief affects stepparents. Fran and I would each facilitate a sharing session—hers on murder and mine on spirituality.

During one of the plenary sessions, a woman named Sonia spoke. Short and clearly Hispanic, Sonia had grey-streaked hair that she ruffled with both hands, laughing and joking that she hoped to get us to think in a different way. A Cuban-American nurse who served in the Vietnam war, Sonia discussed forming relationships with people in mourning who might be different or see things from a different perspective. "Good intentions are not enough if we are different. Slow down, and get to know the person."

Sonia presented a series of steps she believes are necessary to achieve real communcation with the bereaved.

She talked about knowing and appreciating yourself, and cautioned against thinking we have *the* truth. We should recognize that others might have a different filter on our lenses, and while others may think differently, we don't need to give up how we think.

Then she announced to the 600 or so listening that she is a lesbian. "I tell you this because the more I understand and value me, the easier it will be for me to value others."

Her speech was for the benefit of bereaved persons as well as those who work with the bereaved as counselors, clergy and chaplains, and support group facilitators. Her words spoke to the work needed to comfort mourners. At the end, Sonia received a standing ovation.

Later that day I had a chance to talk with her. When I asked her why she announced that she is a lesbian, she replied, "Why do you wear a wedding ring? Everywhere in this conference, I have looked

Hate Is The Sin

and no one is addressing 'partners' or 'significant others' and I think they should."

I agreed and explained that I was a bereaved stepfather and that has not been fully accepted. I also told her about the hate I had experienced in human sexuality discussions, and how that hatred was the main impetus for writing my book.

Sonia explained her own circumstances. Her family is Catholic and her mother wanted her to repent her lesbianism when her father lay dying. She confirmed my observation that the extremes on both sides of the debate were a major source of the hate.

I shared with Sonia a conversation I had with a lesbian partner to a United Methodist pastor. The partner told me the bishop was going to ask about genital contact. We both noted that the churches even treated same-gender abuse as worse than heterosexual abuse.

Sonia talked about people she knew who tried to find a cure for homosexuality, even at a large financial cost.

As we finished talking, I concluded that gays and lesbians are afraid too, but their fear stems from being potential victims.

"It isn't working," Sonia affirmed. "We are polarized by the demonizing that is taking place in this country. That is where your fear is coming from. But the gays and lesbians are afraid, too. Sometimes I think that people who are not secure in their own sexuality can be dangerous. Gay bashing happens all the time."

AM I IN THE WRONG ROOM?

Later at the conference, I went to a workshop that deepened my understanding of the issues Sonia spoke about. The room was separate from the other conference rooms, and I had to walk through a tunnel on the mezzanine floor and down a hallway in a different building. I thought at first it was intentional because the workshop was about AIDS and gay or lesbian parents or children. I later discovered that all other rooms were booked and concluded that I was being overly sensitive.

I walked in and nodded to the three women on the panel. To the left, five rows of chairs faced the speakers. I sat in the second row, close to the door. It soon became clear that I was outnumbered gender-wise, by a margin of twelve to one. I joked to the moderator that I wondered if I was in the right workshop.

"What workshop do you think it is?" she asked.

"AIDS, and gays and lesbians," I replied.

"You're in the right place."

No one was smiling and I was still the only male. My new friend Sonia sat a row behind, in the center.

In the opening remarks, the moderator discussed disenfranchised grief, which is grief that is difficult to talk about in public. Thirty years ago, parents of a child who took his or her life felt shamed by the stigma of suicide. She expressed thanks that suicide no longer carried this shame. AIDS, however, is burdened with that same shame and secrecy and she and others are working to take away the fear and isolation of this bereavement. This was the context of the workshop.

She introduced a woman who identified herself as the mother of a young man who died on a ski trip at age 32. She said she is a lesbian, has been a feminist and an activist in the lesbian and gay community, and now she felt she was just a bereaved mother. She seemed to gain energy as she talked about working with lesbian and gay people who are in mourning.

She described the rejection she experienced from her family and others who could not accept her as a lesbian. She talked about how the support group she belonged to had a motto that all are welcome, but she felt the group only partially tolerated her. Others in the workshop vocally affirmed her concern.

She talked about support groups, noting that despite one hundred people in her group, not one had lost a loved one to AIDS. Once again, I heard the fear of sharing in a group and possibly being condemned.

I could feel a lot of tension in the room. No one smiled, and even efforts at humor brought no joy.

The second panel speaker was a straight woman whose son, a doctor, had taken sick, went into the hospital, and nearly died. When he came home, he said, "Mother, I have something to tell you." She said at first she couldn't comprehend having a gay son with AIDS. She described his life from that point until he died as a life of activism as he tried to put a face on gays. He went on television to talk about the AIDS crisis and about being gay and rejected. As she spoke I heard the undercurrent of her own transformation from shock and disbelief to full acceptance. "At least he didn't die sick, alone, and destitute."

After he died, she started a foundation to carry on his work. "If I have educated and touched people, I have done what my son wanted."

She expressed anger at those who don't accept gays and lesbians as fully human. She personally experienced much of the hate that gays and lesbians face so often. With an exasperated shrug, she added, "I don't understand why ministers have to be so homophobic, with all the violence and other problems in the world. Why fuss about a family with two moms?" This brought applause and affirmations from the group.

Both speakers affirmed that in their minds it is essential to put a face on gay people; to take away the anonymous object of hate and replace it with real human beings. The moderator closed with this thought: "Just by talking about the issue, you are saying you are strong enough to handle the issue."

When I later went over my notes and thought about what I had seen, I realized that I had been the proverbial fly on the wall, listening but not recognized by the others in the room. My status as the only man, and straight as well, made me irrelevant for the women who had suffered the death of a loved one in a society that refused to allow them to grieve openly and without fear. It was safe in the workshop; they could be open without concern for what others might think. I also thought about why it seemed so necessary for each who spoke or asked questions to identify her sexuality. Sexuality was paramount to these women, and I realized it would continue to be important until it truly isn't important to anyone at all. At that workshop, sexuality was accepted as a given, an orientation no one 'chooses' but as part of who individuals are.

A MAN WITH A PARTNER

I wandered a bit, still feeling the intensity of the workshop. Fran had been in a workshop that dealt with transition rituals for when the family pet dies. Our older dog, Rosey, had recently died from liver problems and we were both feeling a bit down. The previous week while I had been at the ELCA Churchwide Assembly, I had called Fran to tell her about the voting. When she answered the phone, I could hear sadness in her voice. She had just come from the veterinarian who told her that nothing could be done for Rosey and they decided to euthanize her.

"I held her, Jack, and told her she would be better now. It was peaceful." I forgot completely about telling her about the vote.

So I was pleased to see Fran smiling after the workshop on pet death. She introduced me to the man who had led the workshop. Fran had been affirmed in what she had done for Rosey, and seemed relieved. The workshop leader talked about his own pets, recalling one of his favorites that he and his partner enjoyed for many years. When Fran and I walked away, I asked her if she heard 'partner' the way I did.

"I don't have a clue," she said. "Ask him."

I went back to the man I will refer to as George, who was standing outside the book store for the conference. "Do you have a little time to talk?" I asked.

"Sure. What's on your mind?"

"You said your partner liked the dog a lot, too?"

"Yes."

"Is your partner a male?"

"Yes. I have been in a committed relationship with my partner for twenty-six years. Why do you ask?"

I told George about my involvement with the ELCA and how I had been troubled by the hate I saw. I asked him if he had an explanation for the hate. He had to have known that same hatred.

"Sure. My mother didn't speak to me for ten years. She was being deprived of grandchildren and would not accept me for who I am. But it is just one form of hate. People hate and despise what is different, what threatens them. When I grew up I experienced absolute hostility. I felt that certain people wanted me dead. I was beat up twice. These guys wanted to beat up someone. They called me a faggot, but they didn't know. It is an attitude. What would we do with the time if we didn't have someone to hate?"

I felt good about talking with George and getting to know him just a little. I thought back to the time when we were conducting the studies before the reports came out, the time I call the "ugly days," when many hurtful things were said. When Pastor Prin asked, "Does everybody agree that homosexuality is not a choice for at least some individuals?" some didn't agree. One person said, "They had an experience as a homosexual and liked it, so they won't change." Many homosexuals live in a constant state of fearing rejection.

George seemed tired as he talked. I felt he appreciated having someone ask about his personal experiences. He smiled. "You know, gays live in constant terror, even if they appear to be fine with being out. This is the first time anyone has ever asked me about the hate I experienced."

George has lived his entire adult life with that constant terror he described to me. I tried to picture him at my home church, perhaps sitting in a pew several rows ahead of me. It is the stated policy of Long Lake Lutheran Church to be welcoming. I could picture a member coming up to George and smiling, shaking his hand, inviting him for coffee in the fellowship hall after the service. Would George mention his partner? Would the church member know what he meant? Then I laughed. I could not imagine George actually coming to Long Lake Lutheran or any other church like it. I had asked him if he went to church and he said, "I'd rather take my chances with God than with any human being."

He talked about his mother and the painful years of separation. "When she died, and the obituary was published, I got five letters from her church right away, then four more and maybe ten altogether. I also got twenty-five cards. Oh, and I got one card from family. Still, I'm always guarded, always pessimistic, and gays I know are distrustful of the church and religion. It isn't that we don't want to believe, but why should we trust the church when they don't accept GLBT folks?"

George was the first gay person I talked with about the so-called gay lifestyle.

"My partner and I have never taken drugs or fooled around. We were at a club where there was beer and hot dogs. Some young kid said, 'Oh look at those two old things. They must have been good sexually because they are still alive.' I said I'd be alive when they are dead. We stay away from the clubs."

I have found that if I talk with someone about their sexuality long enough, he will say, sometimes heatedly, "Do you think I chose this? Did you choose to like women?"

George asked the same question. "There is a battle between the forces of good and evil."

"Like the great last battle of Revelation?" I asked, wondering if he was making a biblical reference.

"Maybe. Listen," he said, shifting his weight as if to change the subject. "Go to a cemetery. What do you read? 'Beloved father, together forever,' that sort of stuff. You will never see 'here lies a faggot' or anything like that. When we're dead, we can't hurt you and you can stop hating. Not you," he said, making it general, not personal. We started to go our separate ways. We each had more things to do at the conference.

George parted with, "When I die, I want my stone to read, 'Wasn't he a nice human being?' My partner will do that for me."

Chapter 12

Did Jesus Approve of Homoerotic Relationships?

In addition to talking with people involved in the human sexuality debate, I found time to read what others have said on the topic. An Episcopal priest, Gray Temple, wrote a book, *Gay Unions: In the Light of Scripture, Tradition and Reason* (2004), that puts forth arguments and reasons in support of sacramental inclusion for gays and lesbians who seek to be in the church. He would approve of Pastor Mary Albing's call to lead LCCR and the Extraordinary Candidacy Project call and ordination of Jay Wiesner at Bethany Lutheran Church. He would also bless their unions with their partners if they were members of his church.

Temple's book uses scripture, tradition, and reason to argue that the heterosexual orientation is no more normal than homosexual orientation, and that anyone seeking a loving, permanent, blessed relationship should, as God's creation, be allowed by the church and by society to do just that. His analysis of the passages that are used to prohibit same-gender relationships is based on a proposition that these texts are centered on the concepts of power and domination, not on sexual orientation. Abuse of power, not relationships, is what is condemned. Temple writes, "In effect, when we read all those passages, sexual and nonsexual, with an understanding of the writer's original intention, gay Christians agree with them right along with the rest of us. Gay Christians and conservatives are snug together on the actual sexual ethics the Bible professes" (p. 82). He also allows for disagreement in interpretation as long as there can be dialogue between those who disagree. Sadly, he finds few instances where such dialogue takes place.

Hate Is The Sin

I found interesting his argument that the Bible has passages that specifically endorse homosexual relationships. He discusses the relationship between David and Saul's son, Jonathan, as being one of love "superior to that of women" and concludes that the writer of First and Second Samuel could have been writing about homoeroticism but more likely the text is about a clear "violation of class boundaries."

Temple also makes an argument that in the Gospel of Matthew (Matt. 8:5-13) Jesus is described as healing a servant of a centurion, yet Matthew "calls the servant a *pais,* street slang for a servant used as a catamite" (p. 86) or a boy kept for unnatural purposes.

After I read Temple's book, I met with New Testament Professor Sarah Henrich, PhD, in her office at Luther Seminary in St. Paul, Minnesota. Sarah warmly greeted me. Only a few inches over five feet tall, she wore a dark purple, long-sleeve sweater and a skirt so long that it reached to the middle of her boots. As part of my introduction, I gave her a copy of my book *Overcoming Grief* (2005) and stated my reasons for writing this current book; partly because I could not understand the hate and partly because I know what happens to people who hate.

I mentioned Temple's treatment of Matt. 8:5-13 to Sarah, saying that the slave was a catamite, or a boy kept for unnatural purposes, as defined by the World Book Dictionary. My computer dictionary defines it as a boy or youth with whom a man has homosexual intercourse. I told her that Temple argues (perhaps I overstated his position) that Jesus approved of a homosexual relationship.

Sarah didn't agree that the text says anything at all about the relationship between the centurion and the slave, adding, "There is nothing in the story that makes that point, and there is no reason to think that is what is going on. It could be that the slave could read, or was a good cook."

Sarah felt that some people trained in systematic theology know better than to take the positions they do, but they do it and it makes her angry. "I can't get my mind into the place of those who come at biblical projects with a clear answer on this or other topics. We are to reengage the text. I relish being Lutheran because we are free to question and to struggle, and I know Presbyterians, Episcopalians, and others do, too."

I named some individuals I have talked with and mentioned how the conservatives won't let me start with orientation. I have to start with the sexual practices.

"I think you do start with orientation. I can't approve some sexual practices, straight or gay, but we have to understand who we are talking about. Galileo or Copernicus didn't undo my faith. We don't see the earth is flat but that's how the Bible describes the world. We do start with orientation." She fidgeted in her chair, obviously struggling with how to say what she felt.

"Love your neighbor doesn't change, ever, but the definition of neighbor does. It's always changing." She shared how she had performed some clinical pastoral care work a long time ago, before drugs and treatments were available, and she saw how the violently disturbed patients were restrained. "It isn't the same. Homosexuality isn't a disease and you can't make a direct comparison, but how we treated patients then would not be seen as humane now, though it may have been back then. The point is that we know more, and we need to use more. We need to give loving treatment. Know who your neighbor is."

She explained that Jews never did like what we call immoral acts, and saw them as idol worship. "True, the ancient world had an idea of morality, but where does it get us now? Why do people say, 'is it not true that these texts are for all eternity?' It is important to remember that we are doing our best to understand the issues and we won't lose salvation by trying to understand. This applies to both sides, unless they harm the other. This is where the hate is bad, not because they are harming homosexuals, which they are, but because they risk their own salvation. Hating is so contrary to God's law. You can't separate the wheat and the tares because they look too much alike and, even if they are identifiable, their roots are too intertwined. How can we identify who must be removed?"

I wondered how many people who hate the sin even think about what effect that may have on their own salvation. As we talked, I remembered Pastor Howard Skulstad's frustration in the study group at Long Lake Lutheran Church when he asked, "How do we honor the body of Christ when we reject the honest opinions others have on this topic?" Yet time after time people replied, "But it's a sin."

I asked Sarah what she thought was the opposite of fundamentalist. "I think about this, and 'liberal' doesn't work, and I don't like the idea of the opposite being 'secular' at all."

She shifted in her chair again. "What is the opposite of fundamental? Confessional? Evangelical, but not as fundamentalists use it? Confessional, I think. How is the Bible a conversation partner to this God? Haven't we learned something about humankind since the Bible was written? Some orientations do bad things. Adultery is not an orientation but we can use our imagination to act out our fantasies on our actual spouse."

"You mean, regardless of our orientation, we can have fantasies or we can be faithful?" I asked.

"There is the joy of union, and fidelity is the issue. Are we faithful? Love expressed toward another is God's love. To deny this is to deny a human opportunity to flower as a person. Gays and lesbians deserve the opportunity to work at it. The gay lifestyle would be the human lifestyle if heterosexuals didn't have stable relationships and support from society. What is the point of denying it?"

"Word Alone does," I said.

"Why does it matter?" Sarah said, showing frustration. "So very few gays and lesbians want to be among us, and they are an easy minority to pick on, and yet we don't do a thing about blatant sins. It gets us off the hook. It is a big red herring. What do we look like to others? It is not about being church but behaving. Look at the end of Romans, chapters twelve through fifteen."

I did, and found this at Romans 14:13, "Let us therefore no longer pass judgment on one another, but resolve instead never to put a stumbling block or hindrance in the way of another."

95 THESES IN SILENT PROTEST

When I returned from Vancouver, I felt I should speak to those affected by the decisions and non-decisions at Orlando. One of the people who stood silently in protest in the convention center during the debate on the third resolution was Jay Wiesner. Jay had attended the assembly as an observer and worked with the Good Soil people. Throughout the assembly, various members of Good Soil greeted the voting members in the hallways, handing out small ceramic crosses to wear. Many of them stood silently along the wall of the visitor and observer section of the room. Only when I looked their way did their presence enter my consciousness, and it symbolized the invisible gays and lesbians in our church and in our world.

Back in Minneapolis, Jay and I talked about that silent protest.

"I was one of those ninety-five. At this point in my life, I truly believe it is the most courageous thing that I have ever done."

He said he considers himself to be a coward inside. "While walking up to my place, I found my legs getting incredibly heavy and my arms feeling like anvils weighing me down, but for some reason I began to receive strength from somewhere. I believe it was God, so I could make the journey through the hall to stand with my sisters and brothers in Christ. This was the point, where these ninety-five folks were willing to say we will no longer be invisible to you. You shall see our faces. We know you are going to do your business and make decisions about us, but while you do, you must see that we are real." He talked about a woman near the front who cried during the silent protest. She noticed an elderly woman in the protest and moved to give her chair to her so she could sit and rest. "The face of Christ became very real in her actions."

During the Assembly, Presiding Bishop Mark Hanson had suggested all sing two verses of the hymn *Beautiful Savior* before getting back to business.

Remembering that moment, Jay said, "Tears began to stream down my face. My voice quivered and shook as we sang that hymn, one of my most favorite hymns in the canon of hymnody. And I continued to be reminded that we indeed have a beautiful Savior, that we are not saved by the Church, but by Christ."

I told Jay that my initial reaction was disappointment. "Sure, the first amendment to the resolution was defeated, but I still had hope for the original resolution. Resolution number two had the two-thirds vote."

"A number of people are angry that we did what we did," Jay said. "They say we have shot ourselves in the foot by angering people. I can hear this critique, but I also question it. Did not Jesus heal on the Sabbath? Did Jesus not overturn the money changers' tables in the temple? Did Martin Luther not nail ninety-five theses on the door of the Castle Church in Wittenberg? Did these things not cause anger in the people witnessing these liberating actions?"

"It was effective and done in good taste," I admitted. "And I do like the analogy to Luther's ninety-five theses." We sat in his office, neither knowing what to say. Then I said, "So, how is Bethany doing?"

"Bethany has never been a church that has been intimidated by the church hierarchy. Two weeks before Orlando we met with Bishop Johnson and said that nothing is going to change and we are going to keep on with what we're doing. We are, of course, thankful that there is no more discipline. Craig [Johnson] said that in the *Metro Lutheran* newspaper so it isn't confidential. I did have a very collegial conversation with him. The first one [ever], by the way."

"And how are you doing?"

"Very active." He paused. "How am I? I'm very exhausted. For some reason, for the last few months I've been more tired than normal. I have always felt that I'm called to serve the ELCA, but lately I have thought more about throwing in the towel and leaving. I have never set a plan, just wrestled with what would I do. The V & E change failed, but that was good because it was an exception. I don't know what to do. I want to tell the ELCA it is a justice issue." Jay seemed distracted as we talked, interested in the conversation but seeming to want to be somewhere else. The image fit his ministry, serving others and not talking about human sexuality.

He is hung up on hierarchy. "It isn't God's church. The UCC theology is so different. I like the tension of Lutheranism between the congregation and hierarchy. I think it is good. Both/and. I don't like being the object of discussion either," he said, when I mentioned Mary's frustration. "I could have done the ordination quietly, but if there are no witnesses, then there is the lack of gospel for GLBT. It brought people to Bethany, even though we're perceived as an inner-city church. I don't want to behave publicly but I will if it helps others. I'm tired of the church studying me."

I brought up Luther.

"He's an occasional theologian," Jay replied, "and when the occasion demanded it, he did his theology. We need to be open and honest and talking. The study guides were most obnoxious. We've studied self-identified gay and lesbian pastors and that is as far as we've gone. We have avoided heterosexual issues. V & E is broken all the time by pastors."

"True," I said. "I know a Lutheran pastor whose wife left him for another Lutheran pastor, and both pastors participated in a funeral for a child of the first marriage."

"Why don't we look at straight folks? In seminary, many times I knew that seminarians were having sex in their rooms, but they said, 'Don't look at us.' I couldn't bring my partner in, but they could have sex in the dormitory. The ELCA is thirty years behind. We don't have a vocabulary that even includes bisexuals and transsexuals."

It was apparent that Jay had held on to some anger, probably justifiably. Hypocrites bother both of us.

Jay continued. "We're dealing with two separate issues. Sexual orientation and gender identity. I am gay, but I am totally a man. The two are mutually exclusive. We are dealing with core gut issues, with objectification of those who come out. There are hundreds of closeted pastors who are trapped and can't say anything. That's sad."

I asked about his work at Augsburg College. I knew he worked there to generate part of his salary.

"I work at Augsburg College as a counselor for those who come to me. At first the gays said, 'We don't want you here. You are Christian,' but in time they accepted me as more than Christian. I deal with GLBT issues at Augsburg, and when people find out I work in a church, they come with God issues."

Jay got up and took a book from his bookcase. "I had to read this book by Marie M. Fortune in seminary and that was good for me. I learned a lot about boundaries, like not kneeling at the bed of a woman in a hospital during chaplain work. In my office I have a window and a door that is open, even a crack during even the most confidential work, because I understand the power of sexuality. Coming out open to the light. No shadows. Doing things in darkness is dangerous."

After talking with Jay, I read the book, *Love Does No Harm: Sexual Ethics for the Rest of Us* (Fortune, 1995). It is a good resource on boundaries.

I told Jay I enjoyed talking with him. He has fresh ideas about life. I look forward to when we can talk about the church and other issues and leave sexuality out of it—like when I talk with Mary Albing about Palestine, for example, or when we look for good restaurants to try. I also like anyone who pulls a book out of the bookcase during a conversation to illustrate a point.

Chapter 13

Speaking About the Sexuality Resolutions

Not long after the ELCA Churchwide Assembly in Orlando, I had several invitations to speak to adult Sunday school classes at various Lutheran Churches in Minneapolis. I found it interesting that my home church made no such request. Pastor Howard Skulstad later told me he didn't want to reopen the issue, but also confided that some of those most vehemently opposed to homosexuals had resigned from the church.

I spoke at Lake Nokomis Lutheran in south Minneapolis. I arrived early to attend the 8 a.m. service. After the service I went to the adult workshop classroom. I set the eleven-inch-thick book of papers from the Churchwide on a makeshift podium. I wore my voting member badge and the ceramic cross from Good Soil. I was initially concerned because only six elderly people sat in the back row and the only other person was the woman who invited me to talk. But by 9:15, when she introduced me, the chairs were full.

I began by talking about my concern for Lutherans who don't trust the denomination. "If we can't solve pronoun problems, how can we deal with the sexuality of committed couples? The discussion about the new hymnbook revealed a strident minority who object to inclusive language and loss of words such as 'king' and 'Lord' and 'His' and 'He.'"

I displayed the seating diagram and talked about how all the sister synods were paired, and how our sister, the Synod of Louisiana and the Gulf Coast, needed our help now because of hurricane Katrina. We had been lucky enough to have the chance to get to know them. I mentioned the appeal that the synod had begun for disaster aid. The pastor spoke up, saying that Lake Nokomis would contribute.

Hate Is The Sin

I had been asked to speak about the sexuality resolutions. I described how the first resolution dealt with staying together as a denomination, and it passed nicely. It is one thing, however, to vote to get along. It is another to put it into practice. I remarked that the bishops held their conference in April, yet failed to agree on any statement concerning sexuality. I shared that one bishop said the meeting was the most painful thing he'd ever attended.

The second human sexuality resolution dealt with pastoral care for same-gender unions, or it did until someone passed an amendment changing "faithful pastoral care to same-sex couples" to read "faithful pastoral care to all to whom they minister." I explained that some people interpreted the change to be good and inclusive by not making same-sex couples different from anyone else. Others interpreted it as not applying to them because it didn't say "same-sex couples." They argued that it watered down the import of the matter. In practice, pastors can do what they want.

I identified the group that lobbied to defeat the resolutions. "The Solid Rock and Word Alone argument is based on the characterization of sexual practices between same-gender persons as being self-gratification. 'You can't love Jesus if you love your homosexual partner.' They don't have an answer for me when I say I love my female wife in the same way that Pastor Jay Wiesner, for example, loves his partner or Pastor Mary Albing loves her partner. They do say that in Genesis 2, God said that male and female should cling to each other and in Genesis 1 be fruitful and multiply."

The testimonies of people at the Churchwide were compelling and I enjoyed telling thirty people of differing viewpoints that they should all get along. I told about a woman reading a romance novel, feeling attraction for the heroine, and going to church to overcome her sin. The audience laughed, but listened when I said the woman was sincere and should be heard. I told about a man who went through twenty years of reparative therapy that he described as hell, and now is free to be gay; we should listen to him as well. My talk suggested that we have to listen to one another, but not try to persuade one another.

Is it wrong to simply want to get along? If it is a matter of justice, am I siding with people like Jimmy Carter, who argues that people who disagree should remain in community and accept the differences? Or should I side instead with Mary and Jay on the need for full acceptance? Can there be full acceptance and also tolerance for other views? It's possible if we stay as a church.

An elderly, well-dressed gentleman raised his hand. "My son is a big church pastor and is saying that the Solid Rock Lutherans organization is going to organize a 'fellowship of churches' that won't be leaving the denomination but hopes to control it."

"There are two sides," I said, "and staying together is important to both of them." I held up a book in each hand and waved them. "This is *Called Into Ministry,* by Pastor Mary Albing of Lutheran Church of Christ the Redeemer, west of here. And this is *Understanding Homosexuality Perspectives for the Local Church,* by Pastor David Glesne of Redeemer Lutheran Church in Fridley, Minnesota, just north of Minneapolis. They have the same publisher. Pastor Mary, who is in a committed relationship with her partner, advocates for acceptance. Pastor David advocates for maintaining the prohibition of same-gender unions and calling pastors who are in them. It may be helpful to read both."

A man raised his hand. "I'm pretty set in my opinion, but your talk makes me at least listen to the other side."

I closed by sharing I had given a similar talk at Lutheran Church of Christ the Redeemer. Pastor Mary Albing had asked, "Jack, when do you think this will be seen as a justice issue and not about sexuality?"

That is precisely the question to ask.

SOLID ROCK ACHIEVES ITS GOAL?

After the Orlando Assembly, I did some research on the Internet. In December 2005, I went to the Web site for Solid Rock Lutherans. I was surprised to read this, signed by Rev. Roy Harrisville III, executive director:

> To all our supporters and friends,
>
> Solid Rock Lutherans officially ceased operation November 9, 2005. We achieved our goal in preventing changes to the current standards on sexuality and ordination in the ELCA. We could not have done so without the help of all our friends across the country who lent a hand in our mission either by volunteering or through financial contributions. We are equally grateful for the

international support we received. The Holy Spirit, we believe, guided our efforts and will continue to do so in the future. Therefore, "Thank You!" to all of you for your kindness and generosity and for your faithful courage.

This prompted me to go immediately to the Word Alone Web site. It was no surprise that the home page on November 18, 2005 carried the headline, "Metro New York Synod votes openly to ordain 'partnered' homosexuals." The article stated "Metro NY Synod is defying current ELCA regulations and rejecting the 2005 assembly's vote against a proposition that would have allowed for such ordinations, but only through a special approval process."

The ELCA secretary was quoted in the Web article as saying that the resolutions were complicated and would require much study. They would also be considered by the Conference of Bishops of the ELCA, which meets twice a year. The Word Alone reporter also quoted the Metro New York Synod bishop stating that the resolutions were in harmony with ELCA guidelines.

In another article, leaders of an organization known as Lutheran Men in Mission were quoted as protesting the actions of the bishop and his synod assembly. I realized I needed to talk to someone from Word Alone. It came as no surprise to find that Redeemer Lutheran Church in Fridley, Minnesota, was a member church. I called Redeemer's Pastor, David Glesne.

WE'RE NOT GOING ANYWHERE

I met Pastor David Glesne at his church. He had just returned from the local elementary school. We shook hands and went to his office as he told me about a grade school student who had committed suicide two days earlier. "Ten of my staff are over there, and I'm going back when we're done talking."

"Take some time to get settled," I said.

"Relax while I put my coat away."

"What happened?" I asked.

David closed his eyes and said, "A sixth grade boy. The day before yesterday. The kids are traumatized."

"Tell me more," I said. Over twenty years working with the bereaved told me that 'traumatized' didn't begin to describe the emotional mess that those students faced.

"He was a fun kid, they say. He seemed normal. He joked and teased and the others joked and teased with him. He was talking about suicide and no one took him seriously. The kids on his bus joked about it. Some even suggested ways to take his own life."

The boy got off the school bus and killed himself. "He went into the barn and hung himself."

The silence that followed weighed on both of us. I could see David's great sadness at the terrible loss of a young person. He also had the pain of the other children, some who attended his church and looked up to him.

It almost seemed trivial to talk about human sexuality in the face of this kind of tragedy. We reminded each other of events at the Churchwide Assembly last August as a transition to the topic at hand. I thought that if the Church pursued its true mission, providing comfort by being Christ to others, maybe there would be room for Pastor Mary and Pastor David to serve the same church.

"So," I said, to get to the topic, "where is Roy Harrisville now that Solid Rock Lutherans has closed up shop?"

"I haven't heard," David replied. "I haven't spoken with him in a while. I think he was trying to line something up."

"And Word Alone is taking that issue now?"

"Actually Word Alone had a conference and formed two groups. CORE, which is Churches for Reconciliation, will focus on a return to the orthodox Lutheran traditions, and LCCC, Lutheran Congregations of Common Confession, will deal with worship and renewal. CORE will deal with homosexuality."

David explained how the homosexuality issues brought two very different groups together. He used the term 'Evangelical Catholics' to describe those on the East Coast, ELCA but very high church with formal rituals like the use of incense. They were thought to be quite different from the Midwest pietistic Lutherans that moved further than the Roman Catholic practices. "But," he added, "both groups held an historical, biblical view on homosexuality and the two groups came together on it."

"Does that mean that Word Alone is going to stay in the ELCA?"

David smiled. "People have assumed the wrong things about Word Alone. Its Statement of Principles is that it intends to renew and reform the ELCA from within. Well, some people have left the church, but Word Alone is staying. We're not going anywhere."

We chatted a while longer, but our minds were on the suicide. A sixth grader's death is such a tragedy, and puts less serious issues into perspective. Perhaps that is why I could tell David about holding up his book and Mary's book at a speaking engagement and use them as representatives of each side of the debate. He seemed pleased when I quoted a man as not changing his mind but at least being willing to listen to the debate. I also told him about the woman at the Churchwide Assembly who held on to her Missouri Synod views of homosexuality even though she changed her views on divorce and women's ordination. He affirmed my suggestion that she talk with a gay or lesbian about how he or she reads the Bible.

SPREADING THE WORD

When I left David, I took copies of two of his sermons. He had preached a series of twelve sermons on contemporary culture, such as sexuality, drugs, abortion, and racism.

David told me that a church in Colorado consisting of mostly elderly members was closing.

"It was an old ALC church, which was a predecessor Lutheran denomination prior to the merger into the ELCA, and they get to keep the property. I met the pastor in Orlando and he wants to send a copy of my book to every rostered pastor in the ELCA. We might send it to the seminarians."

David said that the money for this would come from the sale of the Colorado property, and that the mailing would include a CD of two of his sermons from that series, both on homosexuality. The tapes were his gift to me.

Chapter 14

The Calm Before the Next Storm

After the churchwide assembly in August 2005, it was a time of peace in the Minneapolis Synod. At synod council and executive meetings, people reported that human sexuality had taken a backseat to everyday topics, such as worship, confirmation classes, even helping the homeless. The voices in the pews were more concerned about the larger church efforts to aid hurricane victims.

Human sexuality issues didn't go away, but no one seemed focused on the fact that the Task Force for ELCA Studies on Sexuality would eventually issue an additional study guide which, added to the first study guides, would be the voice of the denomination. The goal of making a Social Statement on Human Sexuality for consideration at the 2009 Churchwide Assembly from the three study guides, debates, and responses, seemed very far away. Maybe this was the calm before the next storm.

WILL REMUS

The contrast between the 2006 annual meeting of Long Lake Lutheran Church and the previous year's meeting amazed the council. The previous year had a contentious debate about the human sexuality resolutions and a motion to not adjourn until after the churchwide assembly in August. At this meeting, no one from the congregation spoke a word, although some of the previous dissentors no longer attended the church.

We adjourned and the council met briefly to thank those completing their terms, and to elect a new council president, Will Remus. Will is an outdoorsman type, with a full beard, handlebar mustache,

Hate Is The Sin

and long, curly, blond hair with traces of gray. Wearing western attire, Will almost always has a coffee cup in his hand.

Will had been part of the discussions the previous year concerning human sexuality, and I arranged to meet with him away from the church. When we met, he had on a floppy wool hat and corduroy coat, and his usual western shirt and boots.

Will was surprised when I told him I was writing this book and wanted to talk to him about his experiences at Long Lake Lutheran Church.

"I tried and tried to figure out what you wanted to talk to me about, and this sure wasn't it."

I explained my pain over the hate produced at the study sessions, and I wanted to know if he had any insights.

"It started when the synod didn't take a complete stand immediately. Some look at homosexuality of any kind as a sin. The difference is that we repent our sins and some of those people don't."

"I can see differences of opinion existing," I said, "but why the hate? We aren't supposed to hate."

"No, we aren't," he said, showing displeasure. "I think it has been blown way out of proportion. Someone wanted an immediate vote at church council. I was there. They wanted it condemned, and Pastor Howard wouldn't do that. He didn't affirm it either, so that wasn't the issue."

We talked about Pastor Andrew's excellent moderation of the study groups, with him not expressing his opinion nor taking sides. "He said he didn't want us to judge. 'This is to open our minds, not change them,' is the way he put it. Some people want things to be black and white, but the world is gray."

We discussed some of the more strident voices, many of whom have left the church for another congregation. "They left because the synod didn't do enough."

"The synod gets blamed for a lot of things at Long Lake Lutheran Church," I admitted.

"Well, someone should be leading us and I think they are afraid to lose members and contributions. We lost them. Some very influential people left us over this, and that cost us a lot of money."

"I think they are better off where they can have their black and white world."

"You're probably right. I'm open, but not persuaded."

"You had no problem with a lesbian singing on Christmas Eve?"

"None at all. I have no problem with membership."

"That's because you see her as an individual, rather than cataloging her as whatever."

"Well, we all sin, Jack, and if you don't forgive someone else's sin, does God forgive your sins? I wonder about that. I remember during the study groups that one gal quoted verse after verse from the Bible, condemning homosexuals."

"Others read the Bible differently. I say that to a lot of people, and most of them agree, then they tell me that the different reading is wrong."

We spoke a while longer, as the conversation shifted to the future of the church and his work as council president. He seemed relaxed and relieved that the homosexuality study was in the past. There were more important issues for Long Lake Lutheran Church. I felt the calm as well.

A PASTORAL MINISTER OF OUTREACH

In November, 2005, I returned to the University Lutheran Church of Hope for another Caring Families Support Group meeting. A woman opened the meeting, announcing for newcomers that the group was a Lutheran support group that affirms gays and lesbians.

Lois Voss, local contact for the Extraordinary Candidacy Project spoke first, saying that after Orlando they were impatient because of the 'baby steps' that were taken, but they were also thankful that the ELCA didn't go backward. She urged the group to watch for opportunities to "do with the time we have left what God wants us to do." She cautioned us to be aware of suffering throughout the world, and to be agents to alleviate some pain of some people some of the time. Then she introduced the featured speaker.

The speaker, Jen Nagel, is a seminary graduate from Chicago Divinity School, who works at Salem English Lutheran Church in south Minneapolis as pastoral minister-outreach. She is not ordained in the ELCA and has not sought ordination by the ECP as Jay Wiesner did, but is on the ECP roster of approved candidates. She asked a rhetorical question: "What does it mean to be waiting?" She pointed out that it was currently Advent, and we should be asking that very question.

Jen talked about her history, being baptized in the Missouri Synod Lutheran Church, and how her mother left to be part of the ALC, which merged into the ELCA. She told us of an eighth-grade ecumenical Thanksgiving dinner "in the church with the biggest basement." She said she was that young when she thought about being a pastor. "The Lutheran call is very personal, of course, but it also requires community affirmation." She recalled being a senior in high school and reading *The Lutheran* magazine. It was 1989 or 1990 and people in the ELCA were upset about human sexuality. "I asked myself how could a church take a stand in this way? I personally knew nothing about sexuality. I dated some, and I suppose I was asexual. I couldn't see then what I know now. And you can't go back."

While in seminary she corresponded with her candidacy committee, a common practice for candidates. In 1998, she met a woman named Jane McBride and "I thought, Oh, this is scary. I fought it and we tried not to see each other. I asked, am I saying no to God? I'm called to ministry, but I'm also called to this relationship. I asked my candidacy committee to resolve this dual call, to ministry and love. I wrote Bishop Stan Olson, the Southwest Minnesota bishop, who said I should follow the rules, be honest, and upright. I talked to the staff and the committee. I didn't expect approval but didn't want denial."

This approach, of staying in the denomination, working as a pastor, almost, but not ordained to what she rightly believes is a valid call, can be seen as a third way, honoring both a call to ministry and obedience to the church rules that oversee ordination. But it denied her the opportunity to serve the sacraments.

Jen talked about wanting approval and having an interview where that approval was subject to the then-pending possible change in church policy. When it didn't change, she went to ECP and was approved by that rostering body. She has been on the ECP roster of candidates for five years, but has not been ordained. Her church, she said, is dealing with many issues and she would not put them through the stress of an ordination, though she would accept it if they asked.

"My partner is an ordained United Church of Christ pastor and serves a church in Minneapolis. We made our own commitment to each other, not in a church, but just the two of us on the Indiana Dunes along Lake Michigan."

I learned that there were about forty persons on the ECP roster, and Jen is one of the younger ones. Someone asked why she didn't leave the ELCA, and she replied, "I will when I'm ready." To a follow-up question of whether she thought it was time, she said, "I need to stay for now, to speak both in and out on the issue."

EXTRAORDINARY CANDIDATES

I had kept a brochure from the Extraordinary Candidacy Project and so called Lois Voss. Lois is listed on the brochure as the local contact for the Twin Cities.

On a snowy day in February, I met Lois in the lobby of the Minneapolis Church Center where the synod has its offices. Lois dressed for the cold weather, with a cloth coat, scarf and hat, and fleece-lined boots. I had been held up by winter weather traffic and she had been waiting for me. She rose when I came in, and we took one of the stuffed chairs and table arrangements set out for just this kind of meeting.

Lois was direct. "My daughter is a lesbian. At eighteen, she came out to us, and has been out for twenty years. She's thirty-eight," Lois added, doing the math for me. "That's why we've been active in the Extraordinary Candidacy Project."

I showed her the ECP brochure I had taken when Jen Nagel spoke at the support group. I read, "ECP is a support for gay and lesbian Lutherans denied access to the ministry by ELCA policy."

"That's ECP. It was formed in 1993 in response to ELCA policies keeping GLBTs out of the pulpit. We started out in Lutherans Concerned. We're in a RIC church—Edina Community Lutheran Church."

I knew that was retired bishop Darold Beekmann's church. Lois said she knew Tim and Patrick.

"Originally ECP was formed as a local presence, mostly in the Bay Area in California. We are part of a local presence in the Twin Cities, around Luther Seminary. We have a panel that does the local work. Initially the Bay Area panel was the only one, then we formed and there is now a panel in the New England area. The Bay Area is the national panel that oversees our panel, the New England one, and a local panel in the Bay Area. We interview applicants or those thinking of applying before they go to the national panel."

When asked, she said her daughter is not in a Lutheran church. I sensed an unwillingness to talk about her daughter, because she didn't volunteer her name or the relationship, if any, she had with anyone. I asked Lois, "Why is there an emphasis on publicity for ordination?"

"These are extraordinary people," she said, smiling, "and we honor their call despite what the ELCA teaches. We want more of the ELCA to see them as fine people. We're putting a face on sexual minorities and this is most important. They have a continuing struggle. They can't find ministries and we help them get positions like Jen Nagel has. The ELCA is hypocritical, saying GLBT are part of the church but not fully part of it. We're seeing an increase in candidates and there are some who should be added to the ECP roster."

Lois described the ECP roster as a way of giving accountability for the candidates, and it acts as a candidacy committee. She sees the ELCA as changing, gradually, and the votes were encouraging. ECP speaks to groups who are interested in the issue.

She also told me about Good Soil. "Good Soil is a group formed in response to Solid Rock, and includes ECP (who work with pastors and candidates), Lutherans Concerned, Wingspan (in St. Paul), Lutheran Network for Inclusive Vision, and Lutheran Lesbian and Gay Ministries (LLGM). The ELCA put a lot of pastors in difficult situations. Mary Albing is staying on the ELCA roster as long as she can, and many don't go to the ECP roster because they want to stay in the system as long as possible."

I asked her what she does when confronted by someone reading the biblical texts literally?

"I am okay with that and try to talk with them, but I'm not hopeful of being understood." She didn't seem to expect much from a debate over biblical texts.

"What do you see in the future?" I was looking for hope.

"The church is responding to the RIC program, and more are becoming that open, to think about reconciliation with gays and lesbians. RIC churches are now trying to discern, 'What next?' Do we change our constitution? Provide more resources for blessings? Publicize the availability of blessings?"

"Do you see ECP's standards as being as good as the ELCA?"

"Yes. When we interview candidates, we are strict. We want them to talk about their sexuality and talk about coming out. On our roster, half are former clergy taken off the ELCA roster and half are in or just graduated from seminary. They are held to the same standards. Many have lived without being 'out.' We try to convince them not to get married to hide their sexuality. People are coming out earlier. My daughter dated a guy and we were surprised. We later learned he was gay and they went together just to go to parties."

Lois Voss never expected to be an advocate for gay and lesbian acceptance, but she responded positively to her daughter's announced orientation. I admire what she has done by staying in the ELCA and working to support those her denomination excludes from full membership and participation. Lois is working for the future of the church. She shows no hate for those who try to keep gays and lesbians out of the pulpit. When our conversation ended, I wished her well. It is nice to talk with people who seek healing.

Chapter 15

A Council Minus the Bishop

In February 2006, the Minneapolis Area Synod Council met at its regularly scheduled time. Prior to the council meeting, I had exchanged e-mails with Jen Nagel. She wanted the synod council to consider several resolutions passed by the Metro New York Synod in November 2005, in response to the decisions made at the August churchwide assembly in Orlando. In essence, the resolutions emphasize the call to "seek unity in the midst of our disagreements" over matters of sexuality. The focus is to use restraint in discipline against gay and lesbian persons in rostered ministry.

I thought the language of the resolutions walked a tightrope by claiming that the synod had the responsibility for pastoral care and discipline of rostered leaders; not the ELCA as a larger entity. Because of this, the synod was not changing the rules, merely enforcing them in its own vision. The key language, I thought, was that the "Synod does not create new standards for discipline, but does exercise its constitutional duty to provide for the implementation of those standards within this Synod."

The resolutions were submitted to the ELCA's Church Council for approval. The Council received the resolution and referred it to the Office of the Secretary for processing in various units, and requested a report and possible recommendations for its April 2006 meeting.

The resolution caused some interest in the Minneapolis Area Synod. Jen Nagel asked for a meeting with the executive committee at large members to discuss possible options to move the Minneapolis Area Synod toward support for the Metropolitan New York Synod resolution. I was on that committee along with Pastor Morris Wee and Pastor Judith Burgett-Winzig. The meeting was mostly informational and, at the time, we didn't even have a copy of the resolution. We

Hate Is The Sin

agreed that continued conversation would be good, which didn't accomplish much but we were unable to commit to anything else.

At the February 2006 meeting, the matter came to the full Minneapolis Area Synod Council meeting. A copy of the Metro New York resolution was included in the material we all received. Bishop Craig Johnson happened to be on a mission trip to South Africa and could not attend. I suggested that Jen bring the resolution to the full council for discussion and, postpone action until Bishop Johnson returned. During the council meeting, someone offered to table the measure. I explained the dates of forthcoming meetings and observed that the full council was not scheduled to meet until after the ELCA Church Council met and, possibly, acted on the Metro New York action. Someone asked if we could have a special meeting to act, and I suggested that we meet at the Executive Committee meeting date in March. We would use the February Executive Committee meeting to get a sense of what Bishop Johnson and the committee wanted to do.

A few weeks later, Bishop Johnson postponed the February Executive Committee meeting until after the March Conference of Bishops meeting. That way we would know what action, if any, that group would recommend. When Bishop Johnson returned from that meeting, he announced that the bishops had declined to act on the Metro New York Synod resolution. It was not a surprise.

Bishop Johnson also brought Pastor Mary Albing's situation and request for an extension of being on leave from call to the Conference of Bishops meeting. The Conference of Bishops did not deny Bishop Johnson's request to keep Mary Albing on the list of rostered pastors on leave from call. Instead, they postponed the decision until the next Conference of Bishops meeting in October 2006. Mary considered sending each of the sixty-five presiding bishops a copy of her book, *Called Into Ministry: To Be a Good and Faithful Pastor.* It would give her a chance to advocate for herself by telling the story of her honest and sincere belief that she is a pastor called by God to serve congregations.

ANOTHER RESOLUTION

Others were actively trying to move the ELCA and the Minneapolis Area Synod to a more accepting position of gays and lesbians who affirmed a call to ministry while in a committed same-gender relationship. Pastor Mary Albing of LCCR and her congregation drafted a resolution that directly addressed her now critical situation. The synod had placed her as being on leave from call on the roster of ELCA pastors even though she was serving as LCCR's pastor.

The initial plan had been to keep her as a rostered pastor on leave from call until the 2005 Churchwide Assembly addressed the issues of partnered pastors seeking a call. Unfortunately, the resolution that would have allowed the bishop to approve her call to LCCR did not pass. Mary and the leaders of LCCR were in a quandary. The congregation council wrote and passed a resolution which, in essence, spoke only to her circumstances at LCCR. Although the resolution passed, it was modified to be generic for any pastor on leave from call solely because of a committed same-gender relationship. Currently, Mary is the only pastor in the Minneapolis Area Synod whose circumstances fit the passed resolution.

I asked Mary if she was satisfied with this resolution.

"Basically the request is to continue my punishment. The executive committee should review and endorse it, I hope. My request to extend the leave from call status should be sent to the Conference of Bishops, who probably will say no. Then the resolution can come to the Minneapolis Area Synod Assembly which can say yes. Can you believe I've been asked to run and be voted on to the Partnership Table (a committee of the synod) as a clergy member? How does the synod do that?"

I didn't know. Her term on the Partnership Table would be for two years, far past the possible end of her status as on leave from call.

"Do you know what else they did? They made me Dean of the South Minneapolis Conference."

I didn't know what to say. A conference is a subdivision of a synod in which geographically associated churches are grouped. Each conference has a representative to the synod council. The dean of a conference can only be a rostered clergy person, presiding at conference events such as the conference assembly. Deans meet regularly with the bishop to exchange news and advice. I saw her appointment to dean as one more effort to support her and to give the bishop additional reasons to extend her ordained status.

With the news that the Conference of Bishops had postponed ruling on our synod council request to extend Mary's call, I wondered at the effect this would have at the synod assembly in April. After all, the decision had been postponed and some would argue that action on the LCCR resolution should wait. Some might even see it as disregarding the need for a decision by the bishops.

TO WORSHIP AND BE WELCOMED

I occasionally talk with Colleen Johnson at Long Lake Lutheran, and we sometimes get together in a social setting. During the 2005 Super Bowl, my wife and I met Colleen and her son and his partner at a restaurant for dinner. They had just returned from Nicaragua and wanted to show us their photos; Fran and I had been there in the late 1980s and early 1990s. We talked and laughed and remembered for three-and-a-half hours, and left the restaurant with dreams of returning to Nicaragua.

Later, at one of the briefings held by the Minneapolis Area Synod for the ELCA voting members, I told several small groups about the dinner. I described the gay partners's relationship that has lasted for over fourteen years. I said that when Fran and I went home, we didn't think about what the other couple might do when they returned to their house and I don't believe they thought about what Fran and I might do. The gender of the couples had absolutely no relevance for the time we spent together. I wondered why this can't be the norm for couple interactions. It is the norm for us.

Another time, my wife and I were invited to the couple's home, partly because the house was new, and partly because Padre Fernando Cardinal, a Jesuit priest and close family friend from Nicaragua, would be their guest for dinner. I had met Padre Fernando in 1986 when I traveled to Nicaragua with a church group, but he did not remember me any more than one of the many other North Americans who had descended on that nation during the Contra war.

We were greeted with hugs and ushered into the kitchen where they had set out a cheese tray and a pot of spicy meatballs. Colleen seemed so proud of her son and gave us a tour of the first floor. The living and dining room were open and not yet furnished, although they had hung art work from Nicaragua and other places. I noticed a poster from a 1980 Picasso exhibit at the Walker Art Center in Minneapolis, and remarked that I had been to that show. The second floor had four bedrooms and two baths, but we did not go up.

Some of the partner's relatives were already there and we waited for Padre Fernando to return. The priest had preached at a Lutheran church in the north Minneapolis suburb of Anoka.

One of the partners told me that he and the other partner had talked in their car on the way back from the service. "I really enjoyed it," he said. "I don't go to church. I've been hurt too many times. I don't get anything out of it. But (the partner) misses church. He was raised Catholic and he misses the spirituality. Not the Catholic Church so much. I wish I could find a church."

"There are some," I said. I told him about Pastor Mary and how the congregation doesn't see her as a lesbian, only as their pastor. "They have two families from the hurricane flooding in Louisiana. They support Habitat for Humanity. They do a lot of social justice things, but the worship is good. Very good music and I feel like I've been to church."

"I don't want a place where they tell me everything I want to hear," he said, nodding knowingly.

"There are a lot of strong-willed people there. Don't worry." I told him about the experiences of a lesbian pastor in St. Paul and how the church where she served was growing, as though those who needed church had found a place to be safe. I mentioned Bishop Beekmann and he laughed and said he knew Patrick and Tim. I promised to help him find a church where he and his partner would be able to worship and be welcomed.

Sadly, each time I suggested that they join us for worship at Pastor Mary Albing's church, they found an excuse not to attend. When I asked Colleen what I should do, she said that her son had been hurt by the church so many times and he didn't want to again be exposed to that pain. The memories are so strong. More sadly, Colleen, who had valued worship at church, stopped inviting her son to attend any church, even a church where he would most certainly be welcome. Clearly her son is one of those Lutherans who Jay Wiesner describes as de-churched. How sad what hate has done.

FRIENDS ON BOTH SIDES OF THE DEBATE

Some time later my wife and I took Colleen to LCCR for a worship service. The music sounded so good, and Pastor Mary's sermon offered comfort and hope. After worship, we went downstairs for coffee and were welcomed as family. On the ride home, Colleen said she doesn't like her home church as much anymore. Too much hate. The interesting thing is that gay and lesbian issues didn't exist at LCCR that Sunday—just good worship.

When we were at LCCR, I learned that the church would be having a Mardi Gras party on the Saturday evening before Ash Wednesday, so I bought two tickets. As it turned out, one of our granddaughters, age seventeen, wanted to stay with us for a week while her parents and another couple took a vacation. I got another ticket for her.

We went to the five o'clock worship service, then downstairs for the party. We sat at a table for eight. My granddaughter sat next to Fran, and Pastor Mary sat next to her with her partner Jane on her other side. As it happened, Ruth Peterson sat on my other side. Ruth had been the LCCR council president when the church called Mary to be pastor. We had a wonderful time with great food, great music, and lots of humor. On the way home, I asked my granddaughter if she knew that Mary and Jane were partners. Lesbian partners.

"I didn't notice," she said. "But it doesn't matter."

She said she knew some gay and lesbian people in high school. She didn't care, and only judged people on how they treated her and others. I was reminded of the young woman at the Orlando churchwide assembly who told us that she and the other youth present were not the future church but the present church. She, of course, was urging inclusiveness.

In researching this book, I have made friends on both sides of the debate, and I have learned so much more about them than simply their views on Leviticus. This is not a surprise. The first time I met Pastor Mary she said, "Many people say that their minds were changed when they met gays and lesbians. We look at God as so generous— what applies to the majority applies to all. You can't convince people it isn't a sin, and they won't change their minds simply by you saying anything, but give them a chance to know the humanity of others and they will change."

Chapter 16

Evangelical or Not?

During the churchwide assembly in August 2005 someone, perhaps Presiding Bishop Mark Hanson or Churchwide Secretary Lowell Almen, said that we were called the Evangelical Lutheran Church in America, and that the first syllable of Evangelical is 'A', as in 'say,' and that those persons and churches who claim to be evangelical, pronounce the first syllable as 'E,' as in 'see.' The person was making a joke, but implied that the ELCA is different from the more fundamentalist evangelical movement.

While this is only a generalization, I have found that evangelical Christians are more likely to condemn homosexuals, or, at least, not affirm them. The more conservative spokespersons for the religious right, such as Pat Robertson, Jerry Falwell and James Dobson, strongly oppose gay and lesbian rights, especially related to blessed unions and ordination to Word and Sacrament. It is worthwhile to see what the more centrist evangelicals have said about these issues.

When I spoke at an adult education class at a Lutheran church after the churchwide assembly, the moderator gave me a copy of Tony Campolo's book *Speaking My Mind* (2004), because Campolo was scheduled to speak there soon. I knew Tony in the 1980s when he was on the National Board of Habitat for Humanity and I was active in the Philadelphia affiliate.

Chapter Four of Campolo's book asks the question, "Is Evangelicalism Sexist?" The chapter relates his experience in speaking his mind that women should not be barred from the pulpit as the Southern Baptist Convention had done. Tony reviews some of the Scriptures, citing 1 Timothy 2:11-12 that states that women should not be allowed to teach in the church. Then he references the preceding section of that text, at 2:9, that women should not wear gold. Then he writes, "I suppose that a literal interpretation of what Paul wrote in

Hate Is The Sin

these verses would also have to apply to the wearing of wedding rings. I applaud the Amish for their consistency, even if I do not agree with their ordering the abolition of wedding rings from the fingers of their church members" (p. 37). Tony does not want a literal interpretation to keep women out of the pulpit.

Chapter Five asks, "Are Evangelicals Handling the Gay Issue All Wrong?" Here Tony acknowledges the tension and strife in the Evangelical world and other denominations, and recognizes that some on both sides tend to demonize the other. He illustrates his own family struggle, writing, "My wife, Peggy, believes that the church should legitimize gay marriages because she thinks that lifelong commitments by people who love each other enhance their humanity. I hold to a more conservative view, believing that same-gender eroticism cannot be reconciled with Scripture" (p. 55). The contrast between Peggy's choice of "love" and Tony's "gender eroticism" is interesting. Word choices frame the debate, even in one's family.

The rest of the chapter explores various positions taken by Evangelicals and others. He makes the same distinction between orientation and behavior that Pastor David Glesne and Dr. Roy Harrisville of Solid Rock made. Campolo states that the "Bible talks only about homosexual *behavior.* It does not deal with *orientation*" (p. 57). He praises those "Christians with homosexual orientations who fight against homosexual behavior through the power of the Holy Spirit" (p. 58). Campolo espouses the argument that many evangelicals make, that orientation and behavior are separate. Implicit in this premise is orientation is God-given but behavior is God-forbidden. I see this as an attempt to support a reading of the texts that justifies the phrase, "Love the sinner but hate the sin." The underlying presumption is that all sexual activity between same-sex oriented persons is a sin. Thus we can hate that sin.

Campolo desires reconciliation between the church and persons of homosexual orientation. He is rightly concerned that the church has not been kind. Unfortunately, in this book he can't get past his interpretation of the Scriptures. He does not hate persons who have homosexual orientations, and yet, in my opinion, he doesn't accept the way they read the same texts.

The persons of homosexual orientation Campolo writes about are those who win "painful inner battles" over their sexual identity. He cites and praises Henri Nouwen as a celibate gay who "did the right thing." Campolo does not address those who, like his wife, believe that "lifelong commitments by people who love each other enhance their humanity." I wondered if Campolo attended a worship service led by Pastor Mary Albing or Pastor Jay Wiesner, would he think about what they do in the privacy of their bedrooms? Does he wonder what straight pastors do in their bedrooms? Since I have worked with Campolo and know he is a decent person, I don't think bedrooms would even enter his mind at a worship service. He doesn't object to women pastors—so is Campolo being selective about which "sins" he finds in Scripture and which he sees are no longer relevant for today? Isn't the use of selective texts not only bad theology but evidence of a different agenda?

WHAT DO OTHER EVANGELICALS SAY?

Another evangelical, Philip Yancey, editor-at-large for the magazine *Christianity Today,* acknowledges that some Christians pursue an agenda of hate for homosexuals. In his book *The Jesus I Never Knew* (1995), Yancey admits that Christians can be selective about the sins they hate. "Nowadays many of the same Christians who hotly condemn homosexuality, which Jesus did not mention, disregard his straightforward commands against divorce. We keep redefining sin and changing the emphasis" (p. 259).

If that was all Yancey said, one might conclude that he would side with Peggy Campolo, not Tony. Yancey tells of seeing a play based on stories from a support group comprised of people with AIDS. He notes that the theater director only decided to stage the play after learning that a local minister celebrated the obituaries of young single men as a sign of God's disapproval. "Increasingly, I fear the church is viewed as an enemy of sinners" (p. 259). Yancey suggests that conflict in the world is not rich versus poor or other such divides, but between "Anything goes" and "Oh, no you don't!" (p. 260).

The issues that divide us also polarize us. He quotes Salman Rushdie as saying the battle of history is fought between the epicures and the puritans. Then he asks, "How to embrace the sinner without encouraging sin?" Yancey, like other evangelicals, cannot get past the "sin" of being homosexual. I interpret him as saying it is not possible to love the sinner and hate the sin. Many GLBT persons I have met would agree.

Yancey has another book that addresses homosexuality from an evangelical perspective. *What's So Amazing About Grace?* (1997) presents a friend of Yancey who has a wife, two children, and a teaching position at an evangelical seminary yet comes out of the closet. Yancy dodges the issue, writing, "I should make it clear that I have no desire to delve into the theological and moral issues surrounding homosexuality, important as they may be. I write about Mel for one reason only: my friendship with him has strongly challenged my notion of how grace should affect my attitude toward 'different' people, even when those differences are serious and perhaps unresolvable" (p. 163).

This story focuses on the struggle this individual had, swinging from random promiscuity to returning to his wife, and finally ending in a committed, monogamous gay relationship. Yancy notes that Mel wanted to know "why Christians highlighted any reference to same-sex unions while disregarding other behavior mentioned in the same passages" (p. 162).

When attending a weekend gay march in Washington, DC, Yancey discovered that gays and lesbians were treated poorly by so many in the evangelical churches that they formed their own church. "Every gay person I interviewed could tell hair-raising tales of rejection, hatred and persecution" (p. 166). Mel's struggle with his relationship with the evangelical church, with examples of rejection and hatred, is compelling. But it is unresolved because Yancey maintains a distinction between the person's orientation, which he and many others believe is not a matter of choice, and behavior, which he and many others believe is a matter of choice.

Yancey states: "The more theologically inclined gay people I interviewed interpret the biblical passages on homosexuality differently. Some of them told me they had offered to sit down and discuss these differences with conservative scholars, but no one had agreed" (p. 166). During my own conversations with theologically inclined gay people, I found that many don't see the biblical passages as even addressing homosexuality because orientation was not the issue. They see the passages as addressing the behavior of heterosexual persons.

Yancey made reference to the way that heterosexual divorce has become acceptable, and how those who are divorced and remarried are fully accepted by many evangelicals and other Christians, though not universally so. He may not say it, but this could be read as an acknowledgment that time will also remove homosexual committed unions from the list of unforgiven sins. But at this time in evangelical history, that is not possible. They still hate the sin.

POLITICAL EVANGELICALS

In a book that many progressive Christians read and discussed, Jim Wallis challenges his readers to think and talk about both religion and politics. *God's Politics, Why the Right Gets It Wrong and the Left Doesn't Get It* (2005) has a clearly stated inclusive message. One review described the religious perspective as evangelical Christian and the political viewpoint as traditional in family values and progressive on issues like poverty and social justice.

Wallis addresses most of the political issues facing the United States and the world. He attempts to seek a middle ground in which polarizing positions on both the right and the left are exposed as being exclusive, and thus not real solutions to the concern. He discusses family and community values in a chapter titled "The Ties That Bond." In the first part of this chapter, Wallis castigates wanton sexual behavior, not making a distinction between heterosexual and homosexual promiscuity. He charges that the left has "often misdiagnosed the roots of our social crisis, mostly leaving out the critical dimension of family breakdown as a fundamental component of problems like poverty and violence" (p. 331).

He asserts that a critical mass of healthy families is essential. Then he says, "But the Right has seized on this agenda and turned it into a mean-spirited crusade. To say that gay and lesbian people are responsible for the breakdown of the heterosexual family is simply wrong" (p. 331). Seeking the middle, Wallis advocates for justice and compassion. "To be both pro-family and pro-gay civil rights could open up some common ground that might take us forward" (p. 331).

Wallis's book is a worthwhile read due to his objective and thoughtful arguments from many perspectives. Wallis makes no distinction between the sinner and the sin. And that is a refreshing step away from fundamentalism.

DEFINITION OF FUNDAMENTALIST

Former President Jimmy Carter, in the magazine *Christian Century* (September 2005), provided an excellent definition of 'fundamentalist:'

> I would describe fundamentalism as, first of all, a movement led almost invariably by authoritarian males who consider themselves to be superior to others and who have an overwhelming commitment to subjugate women and to dominate their fellow believers. Second, fundamentalists draw clear distinctions between themselves, the true believers, and others. They are convinced they are right and that anyone who contradicts them is inferior and beyond the purview of God's full blessing. (p. 32)

On the ordination of women, Carter suggested the Baptist World Alliance be open both to those who see ordination of women as right and also to those who do not. "There will be two groups in our membership: those who choose to discriminate against women and those who treat them equally with men. This accommodation is necessary, because those of us who are gathered within the sacred confines of the Baptist World Alliance must resist the fundamentalist temptation of rigidity, domination and exclusion" (p. 35).

This is what the ELCA is attempting to do: to find a way for some churches to minister to and fully accept gays and lesbians who are in committed relationships, and for other churches to deny them the opportunity to be blessed by that particular church in that relationship or to be its ministers of Word and Sacrament. This is the thrust of the Metro New York Synod resolution. Using President Carter's definition, however, some ELCA members and pastors "view change, cooperation, negotiation or other efforts to resolve differences as signs of weakness" (p. 32). They continue to oppose the middle ground.

Are those who advocate change just as bad? Not if one listens to Pastor Mary Albing. In a sermon she preached prior to the Synod considering her plea for an extension of time, she talked about the gospel. "Embrace the gospel," she said, "for there will always be other gods. But the gospel is our reality. We should have no idolatry and no immorality. No dualism. Live for the other, not for the self." Mary suggested extremism in either direction is wrong. "Don't judge others and don't excuse everything others do." She used several examples, saying that while food or drink can be abused, we don't abstain. "Holiness is not self-improvement, nor is abstention from what is abused."

When I listened to Mary preach, I felt that she saw herself in that middle ground. She wasn't condemning herself for her relationship with Jane and she wasn't saying that anyone can do absolutely anything with anyone else. She doesn't excuse all behavior and doesn't condemn behavior that is based on genuine love.

Chapter 17

And Then There
Are the Methodists

When I lived in the Philadelphia suburbs in the 1990s, I served on the board of *The Other Side* magazine, and I got to know Chris Paige, who then held the position of publisher. I knew that Chris was in a long-term relationship with a woman and, while I had met Beth at magazine parties and events, I didn't have any reason to talk with Chris about her private life.

Then, in April 2003, Beth came out to the congregation of the United Methodist Church. Beth served as associate pastor and broke the news to her congregation in a sermon titled "Walking in Light." Beth discovered she had a lesbian orientation when she was in college. She began a relationship with Chris and, at the time of her sermon, they had lived together for years. For that reason I was not surprised when I received an e-mail from Chris in August 2004, that quoted her partner, Beth Stroud, as saying,

> I know that, by telling the truth about myself, I risk losing my credentials as an ordained United Methodist minister. And that would be a huge loss for me. But I have realized that not telling the whole truth about myself has been holding me back in my faith. I have come to a place where my discipleship, my walk with Christ, requires telling the whole truth, and paying whatever price truthfulness requires.

The e-mail described how charges were brought against Beth, and that a trial was forthcoming. I followed the news, mostly via e-mail but also in newspaper reports. In December 2004, a jury made up of United Methodist Church clergy convicted Beth of violating church law by openly living with her partner in a committed relationship. Methodist law bars "self-avowed, practicing homosexuals" from

Hate Is The Sin

ministry, the story said. Nine votes were necessary for a conviction and the jury voted 12-1 to find her guilty.

Beth appealed the verdict and won a temporary reversal at an intermediate court, the Northeast Jurisdiction Committee on Appeals. The denomination then took the case to the United Methodist Judicial Council, which reversed that ruling and restored the original trial court verdict that had resulted in the minister losing her clergy credentials. No further appeals were possible.

The Judicial Council ruled that Paragraph 304.2 of the Book of Discipline "is not directed at the status of being a homosexual or having a particular sexual orientation." The court said the regulation applies to "practicing" homosexuals rather than a person's sexual orientation.

> No provision of the Discipline bars a person with same-sex orientation from the ordained ministry in the United Methodist Church. Rather, Paragraph 304.3 is directed toward those persons who practice that same-sex orientation by engaging in prohibited sexual activity. Likewise, persons who have a heterosexual orientation who practice that orientation in prohibited ways—by not practicing fidelity in marriage and celibacy in singleness as required by Paragraph 304.2—are subject to chargeable offenses.

Once again the distinction between the sin and the sinner was made. It's okay to be gay or lesbian, but not okay to have a loving relationship possibly predetermined by genetics. I learned from Chris Paige that the trial made specific inquiry into "genital contact" and that Beth told the truth.

After the verdict, Beth said

> I'll continue to work at the church as an associate lay pastor as I have been doing (since December). The silver lining out of all this is that by being out of the closet, my partner and I have started the process to become foster parents. We've filed the final papers. So if that works out, I will be taking some maternity leave. That's a joyful thing for us to look forward to.

Late in 2005, I received an announcement that Beth and Chris had adopted an infant.

FULL COMMUNION BETWEEN THE ELCA AND UMC

In that same session of the United Methodist Church's Judicial Council, another decision was rendered that gave me much more concern. In August, 2005, at the Orlando churchwide assembly, ELCA voting members initiated "Interim Eucharistic Sharing" with The United Methodist Church by a vote of 877-60. The agreement fosters mutual prayer, support, and study. It encourages joint services of Holy Communion following guidelines established by both churches. Interim Eucharistic Sharing is a step that many expect will lead to a relationship of full communion. The agreement had already been approved by the Council of Bishops of The United Methodist Church in April 2005.

I didn't think that the defrocking of Beth Stroud would be a sticking point for the continued relationship between these two denominations. The ELCA clearly has a similar requirement for celibacy of clergy who are not in a heterosexual marriage. What troubled me was a decision by the United Methodist Judicial Council relating to the case of Rev. Ed Johnson, who was serving as senior pastor at South Hill (Va.) United Methodist Church.

The case involved an openly gay man who participated in the South Hill church in a variety of ways, including singing in the choir. The man wanted to transfer his membership from another denomination, and Rev. Johnson began a series of meetings with him. The man's sexual orientation was a significant part of the discussions. Johnson refused to receive the man into membership because he said the man would neither repent nor seek to live a different lifestyle.

The church's associate pastor disagreed with Johnson. This pastor contacted the district superintendent, and a disciplinary process began that eventually resulted in Johnson being placed on involuntary leave by a vote of his fellow ministers at the 2005 clergy session of the Virginia Annual Conference. The decision by the Judicial Council seemed based on an interpretation of the rules where a pastor, who functions as the administrative officer of the particular church, "may" allow a person to join that church but can't be forced to do so. Once again the distinction was made between orientation and practice, seemingly hating the sin so much as to deny the person membership in a congregation.

One magazine reported that the ruling ignited conflict over homosexuality. People on both sides advocated and explained how the church polity clearly supports their position, either that the pastor can or cannot exclude homosexuals just for that reason. A new group was created out of this uproar, calling themselves "Here We Stand." It is comprised of concerned clergy and laity who seek to reverse the denomination's Judicial Council ruling.

In a sermon preached days after the Judicial Council ruling, the senior pastor of a Methodist Church in Minneapolis called for "radical inclusiveness" to a crowd of more than a thousand. Since I'm not a Methodist, I thought it would be best to talk with one. I called a retired Methodist pastor, Reverend Dwight Haberman, whom I knew because of our common interest in the Holy Land. We met for lunch.

I arrived just before Dwight. He came up to my table smiling, plopping a pile of photographs on the table, and setting the books he carried on top of the menu. Although retired, he remains active by preaching some Sundays and filling in where needed. He wore a Habitat for Humanity sweatshirt and a baseball cap with a UPS logo. His short, full beard shined white. He showed me photos of his cabin in northern Minnesota, and then brought out some of a trip he made to Wyoming.

I told him about my book and my concerns regarding the United Methodist Church, and the decision its highest judiciary court had recently affirmed by allowing a pastor to refuse membership in his congregation.

Dwight frowned. "The UMC does some things that hurt me, but it is my denomination. I will probably always be there."

The last time I met Dwight, he mentioned that he had twin sons, one of whom is also a UMC pastor and the other is gay. At the time, we were in mixed company, which didn't allow for the opportunity to talk more about his sons.

"I guess Mark was about forty when he came out," Dwight revealed. "He was the music director in a UMC parish. He now lives about a block from his ex-wife. They divorced and she has remarried. There is still one son at home, in high school. Mark also left his job. The pastor was okay with him, but Mark felt it was like a powder keg. One family could set it off. He's pieced together some socially significant jobs and is getting along."

I asked Dwight how the twin brother reacted. "Did he know?"

"I assume you mean, did he know Mark was gay? To my knowledge, he did not know. He accepted his brother from the beginning. He always has and I believe he always will. He feels, as I do, that Mark has an integrity that awes him. At the same time he is conflicted about the basis of homosexuality. The 'issue' is a white elephant between the two. But he is able to set aside his personal internal conflict. For him the relationship is more important than the issue. They really connect when they are together." Dwight is a proud and loving father, and it showed as he talked about his sons.

"Mark's twin is the pastor of a United Methodist church and his wife is conflicted. She admires Mark, but she considers homosexuality a sin."

We ordered lunch, talked about other interests, and then Dwight came back to his son. "Mark was fully ordained as a deacon in the United Methodist Church and served as secretary to the Board of Ordained Ministry in the Washington and Northern Idaho Conference. Over time he shared with some of the board that he was gay and he felt it was not an issue for a number of board members. When he surrendered his credentials as a deacon, it just about tore my heart out."

"He voluntarily sent them back?"

"Yes. His journey has been so painful. I don't understand the hate. You know," he said, pausing, "if you put ten gays in a room with ten straight guys, I believe the gays would be much more sensitive and caring. That's what pastors are supposed to be."

"Where does the Bible come in? A lot of folks throw biblical texts around."

Dwight smiled for the first time in a while. "I divide the Bible into three parts: Old Testament, Paul and the other New Testament writings, and Jesus' words, in the gospels mostly. Paul trumps the Old Testament, and Jesus trumps Paul and the Old Testament. So what Jesus said about homosexuality is what counts. And Jesus said nothing about it."

Dwight had the last word. "We live in a culture of fear. Mark is fifty, and is so committed to the way he deals with people. But he's at the mercy of those people."

The decision allowing Pastor Johnson to refuse membership in a United Methodist congregation is of real concern to the ELCA. The ELCA's official policy is that GLBT people cannot be denied congregational membership because of same-sex orientation or behavior.

What its reaction will be to the UMC Judicial Council ruling remains to be seen.

A SYMBOL FOR SOME OTHER FEAR

I still didn't have an answer as to where the hate comes from. I haven't met any of the truly militant GLBT advocates, and have only been to one gay pride event. I have been informed that many advocates are wary to open up about their human sexuality; I would need to be "screened" to see if I held common prejudices. On the other side, homophobia shows up from time to time, especially during debates and group discussions. Those adamant about hating the sin talk about the distinction between orientation and behavior with so much animation that I wonder what it is about behavior that is so abhorrent.

We all have things in our lives that we consider to be evil. Adolph Hitler is one person my generation has used as a symbol of evil, far more frequently than other ruthless dictators who ruled with terror. When I see photos of Hitler, I am repulsed, knowing how many innocent people suffered and died because of him. Recently, however, I watched a television program about the German theologian Deitrich Bonhoeffer and there were film clips of Hitler. Maybe because I have been thinking about hate as I worked on this book, I initially felt a very negative emotional response to Hitler's image. Then as Hitler gestured and moved around, as his personality was expressed, his humanness made me pause. Hitler was a human being, I thought, almost saying it out loud.

I don't really hate Hitler. In my grief work over the past twenty plus years, if one does not think of someone for weeks or months on end, one does not hate that person, even if that person murdered a loved one. I had placed Hitler on an abstract shelf in my mind where evil persons belong, not as human but as a reminder of how inhumane humanity can be at times to whole classes of people. As I watched Bonhoeffer struggle on television with the evil he saw, I remembered that Hitler persecuted homosexuals as well as Jews, gypsies, and others he considered less than human.

Hitler has been on other minds as they consider the divisiveness in the debate over human sexuality. Episcopal Bishop John Shelby Spong published an essay in the January/February 2006 issue of *Zion's Herald,* a bimonthly magazine originally associated with the

United Methodist Church but now seen as a progressive Christian voice. Spong claims that the prejudice and attacks expressed toward gays and lesbians "today serve the same political purpose that attacks on Jews served in that earlier [1930s Germany under Hitler] time" (p. 20). Spong comments on a report from the Vatican that announced a "purge" of all gay candidates for the Catholic priesthood.

No conservative, Spong asserts that "One's behavior is no longer to be the basis of judgment. People are now removed because of who they are" (p. 20). This, he says, is what Hitler did to the Jews. Just being Jewish was cause for death. He points out that Hitler blamed the depression in the 1930s on "Jewish bankers" and says that "Political and religious leaders in America today blame homosexual people for the breakdown in family values, the rising divorce rate, and the decline of public morality" (p. 20).

I believe Pastor David Glesne when he says that he does not fear homosexuals. He is clear when he says and writes that the church has done much wrong to homosexuals and the church should ask forgiveness for what it has done. Yet when I talked with a woman in my home church about Long Lake Lutheran Church's sexuality study sessions, she explained some of the others who expressed hate: "It is fear for fellow Christians and the church, and where we are going. Is there no condemnation and hell?"

When I looked up "phobia" in one dictionary, I read, "A persistent, abnormal, or irrational fear of a certain thing or group of things" (Word Book, Inc., 2005). One example was a phobia about snakes. When I looked up homophobia in the same dictionary I read, "Fear, dislike, or hatred of homosexuals" (Word Book, Inc., 2005). We fear snakes, irrationally or not, but we fear, dislike, or hate homosexuals. I don't believe I would ever consider having a snake as a pet. However, I do believe that when people who initially dislike, or hate, homosexual behavior become acquainted with gays or lesbians who are faithful to a partner, they can relax and see the person as a person. A lesbian and her sister sang a duet at the Christmas Eve worship service at Long Lake Lutheran Church a month after their mother told the church council her daughter was in a relationship with another woman.

The following year, the same sisters again sang a duet at Christmas Eve service.

Some people no longer attend Long Lake Lutheran Church and have left our church altogether. They still express hate for the sin and denounce the behavior they believe is a terrible sin. Perhaps for them this hate represents something else. Is it, as my friend suggests, a fear that they need a church that represents clear, unambiguous answers on matters of morals and behavior? Does their literal reading of the biblical texts come from fear that if any part of the Bible isn't literally true, then none of it might be true?

Many years ago, a woman admitted as much to me, albeit on a different topic. I asked her if whether or not a snake could talk was essential to her. Her response was, "If the snake didn't talk, maybe it's all a story and Jesus didn't rise from the dead."

That is unfortunate because faith shouldn't be that fragile. Faith shouldn't be so rigid that one's understanding cannot mature. Liberals sometimes comment that conservative faith values are less mature. One woman left a Lutheran church where human sexuality was being discussed, saying "I grew up in the Baptist church and am going back there." Someone else said, "She's going back to her childhood beliefs, too." Our faith, whether liberal, conservative, or some other label, should be seen as deepening, not simply maturing into something else.

It isn't essential to take St. Paul's words (First Corinthians 13:11) to be pejorative. "When I was a child, I spoke like a child, I thought like a child, I reasoned like a child; when I became an adult, I put an end to childish ways." The faith we learn as a child stays with us and grows deeper or fades away if we become de-churched. We should ask questions that occur to us as we grow older and become an adult. Why is there suffering? Where is God in my life today? What does it mean to love my neighbor as myself? Who is my neighbor? Verse 14 suggests that Paul understands more and in the end hopes to fully understand, as he has been understood. Maturity, this suggests, comes from being understood, by God and by others, and this leads us to understand others better.

Chapter 18

A Visit from the Bishop

On April 2, 2006, Bishop Craig Johnson of the Minneapolis Area Synod paid a visit to LCCR. He had been invited by the LCCR council to speak to the adult education class about the status of Pastor Mary Albing and the relationship of LCCR and the ELCA in general. Mary had sent out meeting notices and cancelled the Saturday and early morning worship services so attendance would be maximized. My wife and I arrived just after nine o'clock on that rainy, gray Sunday morning.

LCCR has a relatively small building. The parking lot on the south side was full so I parked on the street, and Fran and I hurried through a light drizzle. Around nine-fifteen, the members of LCCR began to gather in the library. The bishop was down the hall with Mary in her office. Tables were moved out of the way and folding chairs were unfolded and set in rows.

The room began to fill from the back and I remarked to one member that those must be former Baptists. I spoke at a "yoked" church of Baptists and Presbyterians many years ago and all the Baptists sat in back and the Presbyterians sat in the front pews. As former Presbyterians, Fran and I were in the front row. The room filled and more chairs were added.

Bishop Craig Johnson had greeted the two of us before the gathering began, telling Fran that he had read all about her. When she looked puzzled, I told her that I had given the bishop copies of my last two books.

Bishop Johnson waited for the event to begin, sitting at the end of the front row near the window facing the parking lot. Pastor Mary hurried in and out of the room, taking care of last minute details. She seemed tense, and walked a bit more stiffly than I remembered. This was an important event.

Hate Is The Sin

The president of the LCCR council welcomed the crowd. He compared the LCCR to a pilot ship that went into uncharted waters to find the rocks and sand bars, plotting a safe route for larger ships, like the Minneapolis Area Synod captained by Bishop Johnson. He then introduced the bishop.

Bishop Johnson has an engaging smile. His sharply pressed suit made him look every bit the bishop of the largest synod in the ELCA. He began his remarks by saying that his talk had two parts: the strategy of this synod in all its work, and the issues surrounding gays and lesbians seeking ordination or a call to serve in a church.

"I was elected five years ago, but being elected is not enough reason to think one can lead. I got advice right away from several pastors and took a seminar on leadership." The Bishop's major focus has been in building relationships between people to bring about change.

He then talked about the four major projects of the synod. New starts interested this group. The congregation knew the hard work facing the seven new starts Bishop Johnson spoke about. He talked of global mission, being reminded by one member that LCCR had a partner church relationship with Christmas Lutheran Church in Bethlehem. He spoke of outreach and evangelism.

The questions and comments from the group proved once again that LCCR is involved in many of the different ministries of the ELCA as well as with relationships in the local neighborhood. LCCR is clearly not a 'one issue' church, and most certainly is not a 'gay and lesbian' church. Mary's previous statement that her congregation does not see her as a lesbian in the pulpit came to my mind.

Bishop Johnson then shifted his talk to the "gay and lesbian issues that are important to LCCR." He described how Mary and he had several conversations back when LCCR had an interest in finding a pastor. He described the process of the call, being reminded several times by listeners of other facts that were important in the way LCCR felt led, eventually, to call Mary as its pastor.

"I decided that we could live with her being called. I felt the choice was correct when Mary accepted the call here. I just couldn't sign her letter of call. The ELCA constitution won't let me do that. We hoped that by the time the ELCA met in Orlando last year, space would be created for Mary to have her call here recognized. Unfortunately that didn't happen."

Bishop Johnson described other conversations with Mary and the LCCR council. He said that the MAS executive committee and the full synod council approved a request to extend Mary's time being on leave from call until, at least, the church makes some progress in resolving the issues for gays and lesbians seeking to be pastors. He described going to the Conference of Bishops in March 2006, and presenting the request to extend her time on leave from call. He described the case in detail, praising Mary's work as a pastor, noting that the South Minneapolis Conference Assembly elected her as conference dean, a position that only rostered pastors can have. He told the Conference of Bishops that LCCR was in the top ten churches in terms of per-member giving to the synod.

"I also told them right up front that I could not, in good conscience, remove Mary from the roster." The room burst into applause. "Amazingly," Bishop Johnson continued, "they decided to postpone their decision, at least until October. I have since sent a copy of Mary's book to each of the committee members and I have been talking with each one of them."

Mary spoke at this point. "This is the first time anyone has even gotten six months of extended time. It's a first for gay or lesbian pastors."

I had been watching Mary, seeing her expression change as the bishop spoke, more frowns than smiles. Even though Bishop Johnson and her congregation had only praise and good things to say about her, I could see weariness in her face. Occasionally her eyes rolled, and I suspected that she again felt the pain of being the object of a discussion. We were talking about her, even as she sat there, as though she was an object, not a person.

In response to a question, Bishop Johnson said that he didn't have any idea what would happen in October. He speculated that the committee would approve the extension, emphasizing that he was speculating. "But I don't know what the full Conference of Bishops will do. We're split right down the middle." He added that he sensed a change taking place, even after Orlando, August 2005. Finally, Bishop Johnson said that he didn't "think the Conference of Bishops is the problem. They're trying to hold the church together. When I didn't discipline LCCR when you called Mary, I did not get one note of criticism from any of the other bishops. They never said, 'You blew it.' I think change has to come from the churches, not from the top."

IS IT COMING FROM THE CHURCHES?

After the meeting we celebrated Sunday worship in the sanctuary. This service has a time of meditation and prayer before the formal worship, using the *Taizé Songs for Prayer,* with music used at Taizé, an ecumenical community in France. Those who choose to participate join the cantor in singing one of the short songs, pausing for reflection, and repeating the process several more times. We sang *Bless the Lord My Soul,* and thought about the genuine desire to affirm the ministry of this church.

After the call to worship, Mary invited Bishop Johnson to speak to the congregation, and he reaffirmed in summary what he had said in the adult education class. He stayed through the worship and took communion from Mary, who had consecrated the bread and wine in good Lutheran tradition.

That afternoon happened to be the same day on which the eleven conferences that make up the Minneapolis Area Synod were to meet for a pre-assembly regional gathering at one of four locations in the area. I represent the Northern Conference on the MAS Council and was expected to attend the joint gathering of the Northern and Northwestern Conferences at Central Lutheran Church in Elk River. All pastors and lay persons designated as voting members for the forthcoming Minneapolis Area Synod Assembly were to attend.

When I went into the hall where tables had been set up for the meeting, I saw a woman from my home church and I sat with her. We were joined by another woman from Long Lake Lutheran and senior pastor, Howard Skulstad. Others we knew sat with us. Because I attend a monthly lunch for the clergy of the Northern Conference, I knew the pastors. They are a diverse but faithful group of two women and thirteen men who have been ordained into the ELCA and serve on the roster of the MAS. I knew only two pastors from the Northwest Synod; Pastor Mark Tiede, synod council representative from Northwest, and Pastor David Glesne. David and I greeted each other warmly, and I asked for an update on the suicide that had overshadowed our last meeting.

At Central Lutheran, bishop's associate Glenndy Ose presided. She opened with prayer, spent some time giving an orientation on what to expect if any were first-time voting members, then went through each of the resolutions proposed for adoption at the synod assembly. Some of the business was straightforward: support for Luther Seminary in the Twin Cities and immigration issues where both liberal and conservative pastors agreed that the state should not criminalize the work of the church. Then we considered the two Resolutions that addressed human sexuality, numbered RC 2006-6 and RC 2006-7.

The latter resolution had been sponsored initially by the LCCR congregation council. It called for restraint in removing pastors from the roster if they were in committed same-gender relationships and the pastor had been called by a MAS church and was otherwise affirmed in his or her ministry. Both resolutions urged restraint in applying discipline. No one from the Northern Conference spoke or asked questions. Several pastors from Northwest gave speeches about how there could be no deviation from clear Scripture and the need to "say no to one's children as we raise them in love."

Near the end of the discussion, someone from the Northwestern Conference asked Glenndy Ose if the restraint on gays and lesbians for conduct prohibited by the "Visions and Expectations" document was the only place where exceptions would be made? Glenndy explained that "Visions and Expectations" was an eighteen-page document that addressed many issues for pastors and those seeking ordination, such as stewardship, marriage, fidelity, honesty, and commitment. She said she doubted that any pastor was fully compliant in every respect. She added that the prohibition against same-sex unions was the only prohibition that was enforced at all. Someone at our table mentioned "don't ask, don't tell" as also being applied to that provision. I understood the question as, are we going to make an exception for gays and lesbians? Glenndy's answer was that the exception is directed at gays and lesbians as opposed to pastors who don't contribute to their church, who misuse funds, or who have heterosexual affairs with a choir member. There were no further questions or comments on this issue.

WHO IN THE CHURCH SHOULD SPEAK?

At worship one Sunday, one of the Scripture texts came from the eighth chapter of the Book of Acts, particularly verses 30 and 31: "So Philip ran up to it (the Ethiopian eunuch's chariot) and heard him reading the prophet Isaiah. He asked, 'Do you understand what you are reading?' He replied, 'How can I, unless someone guides me?' And he invited Philip to get in and sit beside him."

I don't recall where the preacher went with the text that morning because my own train of thought took off. Many people are reading the Bible on many issues, including human sexuality, and they are not asking this question of themselves. "How can I understand what I am reading, unless someone guides me in interpreting the texts?" Instead, they assert that their reading is sufficient. I recalled the study sessions where people said, "Well if homosexuality is a sin, what is there to debate?" The debate is whether or not one's reading is valid. Where is Philip in our reading?

Professor Sara Henrich, PhD, New Testament professor at Luther Seminary in St. Paul, recently gave a presentation asking that same question.

"How can I understand what I am reading?" Sara said. "As Lutherans, the Bible is the normal norm for our faith, and we are called to attend to it, but the Bible is not the object of our faith. The Bible must not be mistaken for Christ. Jesus is the Word of God, not the Bible."

She explained that "Luther said, 'No pope can tell Lutherans what a text means.' He doesn't mean anyone with a Bible is the equivalent of anyone else." The implication is that those who are learned in ancient languages and who have read the theologians over the millennia, should be Philip to those who would understand the texts for today.

That same day I read an essay in the *New York Review* (May 25, 2006) by Thomas Nagel reviewing *Public Philosophy: Essays on Morality in Politics,* a book by Michael J. Sandel (2006). Nagel describes liberal thought as arguing that—regardless of the moral issues and in our system of rights under the U.S. constitution and laws—the defense of gay rights does not need to debate the morality of homosexuality, but flows solely from the narrower idea that private sexual conduct is not subject to government control.

Nagel then writes,

> But another school of thought, which can be described as progressive but not liberal, holds that those who oppose conservative positions on such issues as abortion and homosexuality should engage directly with conservatives on the first-order moral and religious questions. Proponents of this view argue that in defending rights to abortion and to sexual freedom it is a

political and philosophical mistake to rely on limits to the legitimate scope and grounds of collective control over the individual. Instead, they maintain, defenders of these rights should argue frankly that conservative religious views on sexual morality and abortion are false. (p. 46)

I agree. Some people will continue to hate the sin and love the sinner, to no one's benefit. A clear statement needs to be made that affirms that the activity or behavior in question is not a sin. The gay rights issues before all of the churches should only concern the limited question of whether or not two people of the same gender can enter into a loving, committed relationship that does not constitute sin. This is a narrow issue, but it is important enough to cause people to leave a denomination they grew up in if it does not currently represent their particular opinion.

Continuing this thinking, I decided to find my own Philip to guide me. I went to talk with Bishop Craig Johnson. We met at the Synod Office building at noon and had a cheerful lunch with some staff members. Then we went to his office and began to talk. I had written down something he had said three years ago, and I wondered if he still held to that view.

"You said, 'There is a new model, of seeing two different biblical views as biblically legitimate but not convergent, as it applies to sexual issues.' Do you still think so?"

"No, that isn't what I think. I just wrote an article on the use of proof texts, because I've seen more of that than ever before in the Lutheran Church. It cuts off discussion, and the person sounds like an oracle from God."

We talked about his view of Scripture, using an analogy to a symphony. "Picture the Book of Romans as a theological symphony," he offered. "It divides into movements. The law, then gospel, then Jews and Gentiles, and then a faithful life. You can't listen to one measure of a symphony and pretend you've heard the whole music."

I told him about retired Bishop Darold Beekmann's wish that the ELCA Task Force use the councils in Jerusalem that are described in the Book of Acts.

"I agree with Darold," Craig said. "Long ago, Judaism had to be closed in order to survive. Then Jesus brought a truth that began to emerge that Gentiles were to be included, even to be included as chosen ones. If people hold divergent opinions on what Scripture says on something, one view will emerge as more faithful. As Lutherans, we see this as being more faithful to Christ."

"Like unclean food and circumcision in Acts."

"And other things," Craig added. "In the first century, slavery was accepted. Since then that view has radically changed, of course."

We added a few more radical changes to the list.

"Do you think it is time for another change, on blessing same-gender unions and ordaining and installing those in such a union?" I asked. "More to the point, do you see any problem with doing that if you would not be violating the ELCA Constitution?"

"In time it will happen. Right now I want to hold things together. You know, I have been restrained in disciplining the conservatives, too. There is a church in the Minneapolis Area Synod that called a Baptist minister as its pastor. I left them alone."

"Any predictions on what the Conference of Bishops will do in the fall?" I asked, referring to Pastor Mary Albing's request to have her status as ordained pastor on leave from call extended.

"I don't know. But I'll keep coming back until I find a way to have her continue serving that church. She's a good pastor."

IT IS TIME TO END THE HATE

After more than two years of reading and talking to many people, I've come to my own conclusion: sexual orientation is not a choice but is inherent in each individual. God created everyone in God's image, and while the fall of Adam and Eve may have brought murder and other sins into the world, homosexuals are no more (or less) fallen than heterosexuals. Because God created humanity and the rest of creation, and while there are (far too many) imperfections in that creation at this time, committed, loving relations between two persons is a goal for every human, and can (and should) be done in a manner consistent with the sexual orientation of the individuals.

Thus heterosexual unions, homosexual unions, and celibacy are all acceptable lifestyles as long as the persons in the unions are faithful to their own orientation and that of their partner. If they are unfaithful, promiscuous, or violent—regardless of orientation—it is wrong. A lesbian marrying a straight man (or a gay man marrying a straight woman) is most likely not a union where both partners can live with integrity. I accept the worldview that human sexuality is a given and is within God's creation as we understand it now.

We should be reading the Bible to support a society in which all humans are held to be faithful to a partner, and if there is a separation after time, such as with a divorce, that sin can be repented. The ELCA, the Presbyterian Church (USA), the Roman Catholic Church, the United Methodist Church, the Episcopal Church in America, and every church should be asking its faithful: "Do you understand what you are reading?" Instead of hating the sin and saying love the sinner, we should respond, "How can I, unless someone guides me?"

To end the hate, the ELCA and other denominations must emulate Philip and bring understanding to the people in the pews of its churches. The church must recognize that the Holy Spirit is among us, guiding us, as Jesus promised. John 16:13 says: "When the Spirit of truth comes, he will guide you into all the truth." The church must seek to bring understanding on issues of human sexuality.

During his opening remarks at Orlando in August 2005, Presiding Bishop Mark Hanson said that there is "too much fear of a radical proclamation of the Gospel." Why should there be fear? Why is it radical?

This book is about a small minority. Gays and lesbians want loving, long-term relationships with someone they love. They want to be held accountable before God and their congregations to the same standards as straight couples. They want the same opportunities as straight pastors to preach the gospel, to proclaim Word and Sacrament, to lead others to Christ.

Why can't the ELCA and other denominations be Philip to their members? Why can't the church simply say, "Our members are risking the loss of their own souls by 'hating the sin' because they cannot separate the sin from those who these members call the sinner?"

Hate is the sin, and the churches should say precisely that.

Bibliography

Albing, Mary (2005). *Called into Ministry: To Be a Good and Faithful Pastor.* Minneapolis, MN: Kirk House Press.

Boswell, John (1980). *Christianity, Social Tolerance, and Homosexuality: Gay People in Western Europe from the Beginning of the Christian Era to the Fourteenth Century.* Chicago, IL: University of Chicago Press.

Campolo, Tony (2004). *Speaking My Mind: The Radical Evangelical Prophet Tackles the Tough Issues Christians Are Afraid to Face.* Nashville, TN: W. Publishing Group.

Carter, Jimmy (September 2005). "Back to Fundamentals," *Christian Century,* pp. 32-35.

Fortune, Marie M. (1995). *Love Does No Harm: Sexual Ethics for the Rest of Us.* New York: Continuum International Publishing Group.

Glesne, David (2005). *Understanding Homosexuality: Perspectives for the Local Church.* Minneapolis, MN: Kirk House Press.

Hultgren, Arland J. and Taylor, Walter F. (2003). *Background Essay of Biblical Texts for Use with Part Two.* Evangelical Lutheran Church in America.

Journey Together Faithfully: ELCA Studies on Sexuality: Part One (2002). Evangelical Lutheran Church in America.

Journey Together Faithfully: The Church and Homosexuality Study Guide: Part Two (2003). Evangelical Lutheran Church in America.

Lull, Timothy F. (ed.) (2004). *Martin Luther's Basic Theological Writings.* Minneapolis, MN: Augsburg Fortress.

Muller, Wayne (1996). *How Then Shall We Live?* New York: Bantam Books.

Munday, John S. (2005). *Overcoming Grief: Joining and Participating in Bereavement.* Chicago: ACTA Publications.

Nagel, Thomas (May 25, 2006). "Progressive but Not Liberal," *New York Review,* pp. 45-58.

Oppenheimer, Mark (June 6-12, 2005). *The Washington Post* Book World Section. *Washington Post National Weekly Edition,* p. 33.

Report and Recommendations from the Task Force for Evangelical Lutheran Church in America Studies on Sexuality (2005). Evangelical Lutheran Church in America.

Sandel, Michael J. (2006). *Public Philosophy: Essays on Morality in Politics.* Boston, MA: Harvard University Press.

Hate Is The Sin

Shorto, Russell (June 19, 2005). "What's Their Real Problem with Gay Marriage?," *New York Times Magazine,* pp. 34-67.

Specter, Michael (May 23, 2005). "Higher Risk: A Reporter at Large," *The New Yorker,* 81(14) 38-44.

Spong, John Shelby (January/February 2006). "Is History Repeating Itself?" *Zion's Herald,* pp. 20-21.

Temple, Gray (2004). *Gay Unions: In the Light of Scripture, Tradition and Reason.* New York: Church Publishing.

Via Media Brochure (March 2004). Sarasota, FL: Southwest Florida Via Media.

Wallis, Jim (2005). *God's Politics: Why the Right Gets It Wrong and the Left Doesn't Get It.* San Francisco, CA: HarperSanFrancisco.

Word Alone Web site. www.sldrck.org. Solid Rock Lutherans. Accessed December 2005.

Word Book, Inc. (2005). The Software MacKiev Company.

Yancey, Philip (1997). *What's So Amazing About Grace?* Grand Rapids, MI: Zondervan.

Yancey, Philip (1998). *The Jesus I Never Knew.* Grand Rapids, MI: Zondervan.

Index

Hate Is The Sin